LED BY THE
SPIRIT

Copyright © 2023 by Kent Mattox

Published by Four Rivers Media

All rights reserved. No portion of this book may be reproduced, stored in a retrieval system, or transmitted in any form or by any means—electronic, mechanical, photocopy, recording, scanning, or other—except for brief quotations in critical reviews or articles, without prior written permission of the author.

Scripture quotations are taken from the New King James Version®. Copyright © 1982 by Thomas Nelson. Used by permission. All rights reserved.

For foreign and subsidiary rights, contact the author.

Cover design by Simon Parry
Cover photo by Frank Morris, Studio Shot

ISBN: 978-1-959095-85-9   1 2 3 4 5 6 7 8 9 10

Printed in the United States of America

LED BY THE SPIRIT

WHAT **BENNY HINN** TAUGHT ME
ABOUT EMPOWERED LIVING

KENT MATTOX

CONTENTS

Foreword vii

Introduction 9

PART I.
RECOGNIZING SPIRIT-LED IMPARTATION

CHAPTER 1. **The Spirit Imparts the Supernatural** 15

CHAPTER 2. **The Spirit Imparts Boldness** 31

CHAPTER 3. **The Spirit Imparts Hunger** 49

CHAPTER 4. **The Spirit Imparts the Inevitability of a Personal Relationship** 63

PART II.
ACTIVATING SPIRIT-LED IMPARTATION

CHAPTER 5. **Activation Through Worship** 79

CHAPTER 6. **Activation Through Submission** 91

CHAPTER 7. **Activation Through Generosity** 105

CHAPTER 8. **Activation Through Living Out the Word of God** 121

PART III. ONWARD

CHAPTER 9. **Charting Your Next Chapter** 133

Resources 145

FOREWORD
BY BENNY HINN

Kent Mattox worked with me for many years and is a very precious man, as well as a powerful instrument of God. He was used to be a great blessing and strength to my life. I love him and Beverly.

We've had great experiences together, Kent and I. He traveled with me for a long time. I'll never forget the many times we prayed together. He became my prayer partner, and it seems that everything Kent and I would agree on together in prayer the Lord would answer.

There was a supernatural impartation of understanding given to Kent by the Holy Spirit to serve and protect the anointing on my life and ministry. This does not come by learning, but only by the touch of God upon one's life.

I knew this man when he started, and to see what God has done in him and through him is a great miracle. A great wealth has been deposited in him by the Lord.

As I have sown Kent (if I may say so) into the nations, in being a part of fulfilling God's destiny for his life, I pray that a bountiful harvest of the wealth that is in him is reaped by those to whom he ministers. As you *read Led By The Spirit*, it is my heartfelt desire that through Kent's personal experience and teachings, you will live a blessed life empowered by the Holy Spirit.

—Benny Hinn

INTRODUCTION

I put the car the rental company had provided me in reverse and backed onto the two-lane highway that ran east to west for twenty-three miles across the tiny island that I now called home. My 20th birthday was just a few days ahead, and as I looked to the left and then to the right, I realized that it didn't matter what direction I chose as there would be no familiar face or place in either direction. I chose to turn right onto the road that had just carried me to the resort I would be staying at for the next few months to build the team that I had been sent there to create.

The beach in October was windy and cold; the atmosphere matched my mood. I was 19 years old, alone, and maybe a little homesick. The rest of the leadership team would arrive by week's end but in the meantime, I was on my own and more than a little depressed by the long stretch of road lined only with evergreen trees, adding to the isolation I was already feeling. I knew that in a few miles the small town of Atlantic Beach would come into view, but it was already nine o'clock and was dark in the way that only a pre-winter night in the South can be. There weren't even any fast food restaurants and as my stomach rumbled I realized that the bacon and eggs I had for breakfast were long gone.

As I approached the only traffic light at the four-way stop I had to decide which way to go and in my unfocused state of mind, it made sense to just accelerate and go forward. My first thought after going through the light was that I should have turned left and gone to Morehead City where I knew there were restaurants, but I continued on Salter Path road past all of the shuttered and dark Mom and Pop hotels and food stands that lined the road and that I imagined would be packed during the season; but on this night, mine was the only car on the road. My mood was already melancholy but, in that moment, I felt downright depressed. I was about to turn around when one bright neon light ahead caught my attention, so I accelerated once again and headed straight for that light. In a later chapter in this story, you will understand the significance of that one decision to follow a neon light and just how intentional our God is when He has set destiny in action.

As the car slowed the small, white building came into view. There were three cars in the parking lot and I could feel the bass from the music inside as I stepped out of the car. I briskly rubbed my hands together and drew my shoulders up by my ears to head into the wind that was now really beginning to pick up. As I pushed through the door my eyes adjusted to the dim lighting and I took in the rectangular-shaped bar—one bartender, one customer—now me.

I took a seat with my back to the dance floor in the middle of the long bar and just sat there letting the warmth of the room envelop me. I was still completely on my own but in that moment the girl behind the bar turned toward me and as she looked straight into my eyes there was an internal shift that caused my entire being, spirit, soul, and body to shift. I started paying attention. She looked good but this was something else entirely. The normal course of events took place; she was gracious and professional, and I enjoyed bar snacks and a beer. Nothing extraordinary happened other than the supernatural, unprecedented awareness of this stranger. I left fortified and more confident but didn't think much about that encounter until I found myself in exactly the same place a year later, and this time, everything was different.

Our adventure unfolds throughout the chapters of this book, as the story was written for us long before we knew our part. God had already shown my future wife the plans He had for us and how critical following that one neon light had been for our destinies.

Years later I stood in Wembley Stadium in Brent, London with 50,000 people worshiping God as hundreds of thousands of lights streamed throughout the crusade event illuminating every inch of that place as the glory of God began to flood our hearts. In that moment I could only pour out my gratitude for the many cities and countries where the same anointing that led me to travel the world with Pastor Benny Hinn has illuminated so many souls and brought them from darkness to light. I thought about that 19-year-old boy who was so alone, but followed one light that led him to his destiny and carried him from that tiny island in Atlantic Beach, North Carolina to the lights of Rome, Paris, Jerusalem, London and so many other nations of the world. I was overwhelmed by God's love for His people and for me. I had been led by the Spirit.

PART ONE

RECOGNIZING SPIRIT-LED IMPARTATION

CHAPTER 1

THE SPIRIT IMPARTS THE SUPERNATURAL

In the 80s, my dad walked through a midlife crisis of sorts. Some of it was internal like we typically envision. Some of it was external. In fact, outside factors seemed to cause it.

He had been a fairly successful businessman but through a difficult season, he lost almost all of his wealth. In fact, he had one piece of property remaining in his portfolio.

The land was located near Orlando, so my parents moved to Florida to see if he could develop the site and earn some of his savings back. Without another chapter of success, there's no way he could have ever retired. This was his last shot.

Around this same time, Beverly and I had both encountered the Lord on our own. Both of us were beginning our journey with Him.

After we were saved, we were presented with so many work opportunities. I was offered more money than I'd ever made to go back into sales. Part of me felt like this was the blessing of God, His favor for turning my life around. A bigger part of me, though, sensed that God had something more and that we needed to trust Him and step into the unknown.

We decided to move to Florida with my parents.

My Dad encouraged the move. "Come on," he said. "If something good happens to me, it will happen to you, too!"

It was the mid-80s, and we—a group of five people from Oxford, Alabama—loaded up everything we could and made the drive south. It was a lot like the Beverly Hillbillies.

Looking back, I sense an unseen hand led us the entire time.

SOMETIMES GOD SNEAKS US IN

I knew one guy in the Orlando area. We used to smoke dope together—a lot of dope. When I got saved, the Lord delivered me from my past addictions. That's part of our story. I was an addict and Beverly was a dealer; but, for some reason I ended up calling that old friend as soon as we arrived.

"I can't believe you're down here," he said. Then—"Let's smoke some weed!"

"I don't really do that anymore," I replied.

After asking the customary questions—why we moved, how marriage was going, and why I didn't want to get high—I asked him if he knew of a church I could attend.

"I've been born again, and I need somewhere to plant roots," I told him. That was the term I used—*born again*.

"You've got to be joking!" he said.

I thought he might be pushing back against my stance, but he wasn't. In fact, he actually *helped* me.

"My wife has been born again, too," he said. "She's been going to this radical church down the street. It's led by a guy named Benny Hinn. I've been there with my wife a few times."

He painted the picture quite well of everything you might already envision.

"This church will trip you out," he said. "There are probably thousands of people who attend." He added, "It's really hard to get a seat. People actually wait outside in a long line just hoping to get in."

"Sounds like something we would like to try," I told him, "but it sounds like it won't work out."

Turns out, my friend had a plan.

"I can get you in," he said.

"You just said it was full!"

"It is, but all of the ushers wear burgundy blazers with a logo on them."

Remember, this was back in the 80s. Ushers with jackets were a thing back then—especially at the kind of church you're conjuring in your mind.

"Every time I go I get great seats," he continued. "I've got a suit-coat for work that's almost identical to the ones they have. Whenever I go, I put it on and act like I'm supposed to be there. Then, I head to a good seat." He promised, "I'll handle it!"

Sure enough, he kept his word. A few days later, Dean drove up in his van. He was high when he arrived, pot smoke wafting through the air.

"Is this Cheech and Chong?" I thought.

The furthest thing from my mind was anything about destiny and purpose and walking into the next best chapter of life. But, when you understand the promises of Romans 8:28, where Paul argues that God leverages every circumstance in our lives for our good and His glory, it makes sense that the Creator and Sustainer of all things, who is actively reconciling everything to Himself, actually used this. Yes, a drug addict chauffeured Beverly and me to a church service

led by a man we'd never heard of, and he "faked" his position as an usher and led us to a seat in the middle of the sanctuary.

God knew what He was doing. We might not have found our way in there without all of these seemingly absurd pieces fitting together.

Eventually, Pastor Benny took the stage. The only way to say it is to just state the obvious—I had never seen anything like *that* in my life. Part of him seemed "over the top," yet I could not deny what I felt.

Nor could I shake what I saw. Miracles happened—just like you read about in the Scriptures.

"This is where we need to be," I told Beverly. "We're new in the Lord, and we both desperately want to follow Him."

She agreed.

During the week, we helped my dad develop his property. On Sundays, we drove almost an hour each way to Pastor Benny's church. Many of those weeks my friend's wife drove, making the round trip with us.

THE NIGHT IT ALL BEGAN

One Sunday night about a month into this, I felt God's nearness in a unique way. I remember it clearly. There were about 2,000 people in the auditorium as the service began, but I sensed He had something *for me*.

"You have a plan for me," I prayed. "I'll do anything you want me to do. I just need to know what it is."

Suddenly, Pastor Benny stopped the service. Pleasantly, the room collectively sighed.

He looked up, then locked eyes with me in the back of the sanctuary. "You, young man. Stand up!"

I looked around. Surely, he was speaking to someone else. I mean, I had just finished my prayer no more than 60 seconds ago.

"You," he continued, "the one looking around to see if I'm talking to someone else. I'm speaking to *you*."

I looked to him. He had my attention.

"Is that your wife? You two come down here."

As Beverly and I made the journey from the back of the room towards the platform, a million thoughts floated through my mind. How does this work? Did he know that I had just prayed that prayer? How did he know to call me out of all these hundreds of people?

As we neared him, he said—and you know it marked me when I can still recount the exact words almost four decades later—"the trials of the past have come to an end, and the glory of tomorrow will be revealed to you in clarity. I'll place you in a place of ministry, where wounded lambs will come your way. Not only will you deliver them, but you will strengthen them and you'll see them grow. I will place you in a place of ministry."

"Be strong, says God."

"Be strong, says God."

"Be strong, says God."

Three times . . . four ["Be strong!"]

"I will place you in a place of ministry," he continued, "and nothing will stop Me, says God, from accomplishing my plans for your life."

I looked over to my wife, who was fairly reserved, by the way. For the first time in her life, she laid there, slain in the Spirit—an unusual occurrence in which the person has a profound encounter with the Holy Spirit.

I began to cry, knowing I had encountered the Living God. I had uttered a simple prayer and here was an instant answer.

Someone (probably in a legitimate burgundy blazer) helped us compose ourselves. They sat us on the front row, while Pastor Benny continued ministering to others.

About five minutes later, Pastor made his way back to us and stood in front of me.

"I don't know how," he said, "but you are going to be in the ministry with me. That's what God has called you to do."

More thoughts flooded my mind. Things like, "I don't have any education." "I'm not sure what ministers even do." "I'm a drug addict who just got saved and then snuck into the church building with another drug addict wearing a fake jacket."

MORE THAN A DREAM

We continued attending church on the weekends and helping my dad with his project during the weekdays. I didn't see Pastor Benny much, other than one time when I met with him briefly and shared part of my story, but Beverly and I began volunteering to serve in more areas.

We also began reading the Bible and praying. Both of those practices were new to us. As we grew in the Lord, I often pondered what that prophetic word meant.

But then I saw a glimpse of what it *might* mean. I had a dream. Just like you read about in the Bible.

In the dream, I felt like I was in one of those movies in which the main character runs from destruction—from a quake or storm that's following them. I was in a car with some family and friends.

As we sped towards a place of worship, I cried out, "We've got to get right with God!"

We jumped out of the car, raced into the building, and the destruction passed over us. We were safe.

> **THE LORD ORCHESTRATES THE OBEDIENCE HE REQUIRES.**

I awoke, my heart racing. It felt like it might burst through my chest.

Then God clearly told me, "Preach my Word!"

I asked him, "How do I do that?"

He replied, "See Benny."

This was my first dream-encounter with the Lord. I pondered two things at this moment. First, I'd never communicated with God while I was asleep. That was new.

Second, thousands of people attended the church each week. You don't just walk in the office and "go see Pastor Benny."

Well, I got an answer to both issues.

First, in Acts 2, the Holy Spirit fell on the disciples and others who gathered in the Upper Room on Pentecost. Many of them spoke in other tongues.

When a crowd converged and assumed they were all drunk, Peter reminded them in Acts 2 17-18 (NIV) of something the prophet Joel foretold centuries before:

In the last days, God says, ' I will pour out my Spirit on all people. Your sons and daughters will prophesy, your young men will see visions, your old men will dream dreams. Even on my servants, both men and women, I will pour out my Spirit in those days, and they will prophesy. I will show wonders in the heavens above and signs on the earth below.' —Joel 2:28-30 (NIV)

Second, a few days later, the church hosted a party to thank all the volunteers. As the senior leader, Pastor Benny was there with other staff members.

He approached me.

"You're Kent, right?"

"Yes, sir."

"I feel like the Lord spoke to my wife, Suzanne, and me two nights ago. You're supposed to be a pastor here at the church."

This was the exact night I had my dream. One doesn't just "see Pastor Benny," yet here he was—all under the Lord's instructions. The Lord orchestrates the obedience He requires.

"How does that even work?" I asked Pastor Benny. I reminded him that I wasn't educated and that I had been working with my father. "I've never even read the entire Bible," I added. "I mean, I'm working my way through it, but I haven't finished it yet."

"If it's God," Pastor replied, "it will work out."

He told me to continue doing what I was doing, to keep meeting with the Lord, serving as I felt led, and attending church like I was already doing.

Then, he emphasized, "Come *this* Sunday night."

"I can do that," I said.

"Let's just see what God says—and see what He does," he affirmed.

One of the things I admire about Pastor Benny and the prophetic is the practical simplicity. Often, when people receive a word of prophecy they rush to find something that "fits." They presume they have all of the information they need in that moment.

In Pastor Benny's approach I saw that the Lord could step in and speak to us at any moment; at the same time, it might require some time to understand everything God had in mind in that moment. And, if we rushed to "fulfill the Word" before we had the full counsel of God, we might miss something pertinent to where He was leading.

"YOU'RE NOW A PASTOR"

That weekend, I attended a Sunday evening service—alone. Beverly stayed behind at the house with the kids. I was determined not to miss.

For the second time, Pastor Benny called me up front. This time, he stood me before the congregation and introduced me.

"This is Kent Mattox," he began. "He's one of our new pastors."

Imagine, there I am, standing before 2,000 people. I have no training and no practical experience. I didn't even know before the service that I was about to be a pastor.

When I returned home, I told Beverly, "I'm a pastor now."

"What do you mean? How in the world did that happen?"

She was just as perplexed as I was.

"I don't know," I said. I told her the story as clearly as I could: "Pastor Benny called me up front again, and then he told everyone I was now a pastor at the church."

"Are they going to pay you? Like, is it your job now?"

"I don't know. I didn't think to ask."

What I *did* know was that I was invited to the Monday morning staff meeting. The first time I attended it was obvious I was the odd man in the room.

I scanned the tables, evaluating what all the others were like. They were "real" leaders. Most had been to seminary. They knew how to dress and talk and act. Many of them even led their own churches at some point in the past. Pastor Benny had built a team of well-trained, highly skilled leaders to help carry the load at Orland Christian Center.

During that meeting, someone asked the question to the group, "What's your burden? What has God put on your heart?"

Systematically, person after person began to answer, the conversation moving around the table in the order in which each member was seated.

"China," one man said.

Then the next: "Senior citizens. My heart is for the aged."

"Children," one added, "and the families who are raising them."

I thought to myself, "Oh! I've got to come up with something. I've got to find a burden—*a cause*—fast. My turn is almost here. And it's got to be good—this is my first day as a pastor!"

Again, I felt out of place. Talk about impostor syndrome!

Finally, it was my turn.

"What is it, Mattox?"

That's what Pastor Benny always called me and still calls me—*Mattox*. "I don't have any burdens," I said. "I've cast them all on the Lord!"

The room exploded with laughter.

Pastor looked at me intently. I knew in that moment that, somehow, God created an instant bond between us—a supernatural connection.

"You and I," he said, "are going to be really good friends."

YOU WON'T UNDERSTAND IT . . .
BUT GOD WILL TRAIN YOU

Soon thereafter, I received my first assignment. I was going to be the Singles Pastor. Thankfully, someone was tapped to train me.

However, the onboarding process never happened. The day I met with the previous leader, he walked up to me, handed over a cardboard box full of names, name tags, and assorted items.

"You'll figure it out," he said.

He patted me on the back and walked off, leaving me—and Beverly—to oversee a group of 150 single adults, ranging from ages 18-90. For about a year, that's what we did faithfully, and it was a great place to begin. We continued studying the Scriptures, experienced more of the Holy Spirit, and practically learned what it means to lead a group of people.

Then, the Lord spoke to me.

"Pastor Benny is about to start a crusade and television ministry. This is the reason you've been sent here to help him."

I didn't know anything about crusades or TV, and though Pastor Benny is probably most known for those two facets of his ministry, neither existed when my friend escorted me into the church with his pretend blazer. Back then, Pastor Benny wasn't filling stadiums nor was he a renowned televangelist; he was a pastor leading a local congregation.

A few days later, he called me to his office.

"Mattox, I've been thinking . . . "

"I know what you're going to say, Pastor."

"That's impossible," he replied, "because I want to talk to you about something new, something we haven't done before. Nobody else knows about it except for my wife."

"Well, I know, too."

"What do you think it is?" he asked.

"I *think* the Lord showed me that you're about to begin a crusade ministry and a television ministry..."

"Yes!"

"...and I believe that I'm supposed to help you with it. That's why I'm here."

"Yes to both! How did you know?"

"I've been learning to hear the Lord while I've been here," I said. "I've watched you show me what's possible. I've learned some on my own as I've spent time with Him, also."

"Well, that is exactly what I wanted to talk to you about. This is a shift I'm about to make in our ministry, and I felt impressed that you are the one to help me do it."

Again, when I tell you that I knew *nothing* about cameras and crusades, I mean *nada*. Zip. Zilch.

We began with one camera and a church chair placed in the parking lot at the church. That was literally the first television program. Months later we housed the television ministry in a full studio with too many cameras to count.

Three months after rolling the first video footage, we traveled to a church in Phoenix for the first crusade. Over 3,000 people attended. After that, though, we moved to larger arenas and even outdoors. I watched the crowds swell from 4,000 to 8,000 to massive coliseums. Every month, we filled another stadium of 30,000 to 40,000 people, each wanting to encounter the Lord.

Then, for the next ten years, we circled the globe 250 days a year while also running the television program and leading the local congregation in Orlando.

We hosted four partner conferences each year for supporters of the ministry. We traveled overseas six times a year. We led trips to Israel for 2,000+ people at a time.

THINK BIGGER

Now, I told you the first revelation I received from Pastor Benny was about the supernatural—and God wanted His supernatural power to do its work in my lfie. I was ready to receive the revelation when I arrived. Looking back, that's clear.

However, I needed a teacher—someone to help me learn to navigate that realm of the Spirit, that unseen reality that exists above religion and morality and simply making it through the grind of life.

Pastor Benny showed me that with God we often think too small—that God can do big things. He can operate at a level that, as Paul writes, abundantly exceeds anything we can "ask, think, or imagine" (Ephesians 3:19-20, NKJV).

Here's what stands out to me about all of it, though.

God doesn't always look for the most humanly qualified people. Paul writes about this too in 1 Corinthians 1:26-29 (NIV):

Brothers and sisters, think of what you were when you were called. Not many of you were wise by human standards; not many were influential; not many were of noble birth. But God chose the foolish things of the world to shame the wise; God chose the weak things of the world to shame the strong. God chose the lowly things of this world and the despised things—and the things that are not—to nullify the things that are, so that no one may boast before him.

> **THE CALL OF GOD IS GREATER THAN ANY MAN-MADE CREDENTIAL WE COULD ASPIRE TO.**

Think about it logically.

If God purposes to do something at the capacity of the Kingdom and not the ability of man, then why would human credentials limit Him?

To be clear, it's not that human accolades and awards and achievements don't matter. They do.

In fact, many people are surprised when I tell them Pastor Benny has a doctorate. That's why I often refer to him as "Doc."

At the same time, the call of God is greater than any man-made credential we could aspire to.

Pastor Benny obviously didn't worry about human qualifications, either. If he did, he wouldn't have taken a risk on me.

I wasn't the only one who would have been "unqualified," though.

For example, our crusade director was an ex-mafia enforcer. He encountered the Lord—just like Paul—and did an absolute about-face.

Another personal assistant who traveled with us was an ex-heroin addict. The Lord showed him that there was no high quite like the Most High.

One of our traveling staff members had been homeless. Pastor Benny met him on the sidewalk near the church building. He fed him, offered him some clothing, and helped him find housing. The man was saved, mentored, and then became a servant to the entire team.

To "qualify" in Pastor Benny's mind, you need to have a call, and you need to faithfully pursue it while walking in relationship with others and the Lord. That was enough. In fact, that was all there was, because nothing could top it.

One day he told me he got his inspiration from Kathryn Kuhlman. Most of the men in the choir at her healing meetings were ex-alcoholics. Yet, there they were, leading powerful worship in those crusades. Pastor Benny reminded me often of the scripture, "He that forgiveth much, loveth much."

He had no problem acting on a Word from the Lord—whether it involved a person who should be set in a place of leadership or a project that should be launched—like those crusades and that television ministry.

I gleaned that from him. I discovered, as he demonstrated to me, that the words of Zechariah 4:6 (NKJV) ring true: "It's not by might or power, but by my Spirit, says the Lord."

From my first encounter with Pastor Benny—Doc, as I personally call him—to this present day, I've been able to live in the realm of the supernatural. In fact, as you'll learn later, that's how the church Beverly and I eventually started was birthed.

CHAPTER 2

THE SPIRIT IMPARTS BOLDNESS

I learned how to shepherd and lead and just about everything else pastors do while serving in front of people—not in a classroom. The pastors at Orlando Christian Center always sat onstage. We wore suits and sat turning through the pages of our Bibles as Doc preached.

As we did, I continued fighting that same impostor syndrome I felt in my first staff meeting.

I remember Pastor stepping to the pulpit and directing the congregation, "Turn in your Bibles to the book of . . . "

For the first few months, it didn't matter what book he called out. I was meeting with the Lord during my personal time and reading through the Scriptures—devouring them daily. I still didn't know where the sixty-six books were, though. In fact, I often heard him mention a book and thought, "Hmm . . . I don't know about that one. I wonder where it might be."

The church was on television, so the cameras often panned over the audience—or the pastors onstage—as Pastor Benny paused for people to find the passage. I can't begin to count how many times I acted as if I found the right location, only to sneak my way to the Table of Contents a few minutes into his message! (Pastor Benny is a phenomenal teacher of the Word, by the way, as he's a voracious student of it. I'll tell you about that later.)

SINK OR SWIM

So, yes, I learned my way around the Bible—in large part—by navigating the pages of Scripture while sitting onstage. That is, I found my path in those "sink or swim" moments with everyone watching.

Then there were bigger things I learned—like prophecy and interpretation of tongues. I learned those in odd ways, as well.

For instance, one Sunday evening Pastor Benny stopped preaching in English and began speaking in tongues. By then I'd seen many unusual happenings in the church, but this certainly vied for top position.

"What is this?" I thought. "I've never seen anything like this."

He never interpreted anything. He just walked around for a few minutes speaking in an unknown language.

He eventually approached his wife. It was clear he whispered something to her. She nodded, then looked at me.

Then she stood from her seat and walked my way. I was sitting onstage. As she approached me, I envisioned all the eyes in the room beginning to look to me.

"Pastor Benny just told me that the Lord has forbidden him to speak in English right now. He's going to continue speaking in tongues, and you're going to interpret."

My initial response was to tell her, "I don't even know what this is!" And, "I've never even seen this before, much less actually participated and done it."

I didn't share any of that with her, of course. I just sat there. Shellshocked.

I looked at Pastor Benny. Turns out, she was right. He motioned for me to join him.

I reluctantly rose from my chair, marched down the stairs, and stood near his side.

He grabbed my hand and hurriedly led me through the crowd. He spoke in tongues as we strode down the aisle, hand-in-hand, stopping before a couple.

He let go of my hand and directed them to stand, then began speaking in tongues over them. When he finished, he locked eyes with me.

I said nothing. I just stood there.

He grunted, emphasizing that it was my turn to interpret.

I didn't hear anything from the Lord in that moment. I remember asking myself, "What would be a good starting point? Could I just say something that would sound like something God might say? Maybe that would get me started and open the floodgates or something..."

Still, nothing.

So, I made something up. I spoke a few words that were Biblically and theologically true, I just knew they were absolutely *not* anything remotely related to an interpretation of what Pastor Benny uttered.

Turns out, everyone knew. My words—even though true—fell flat. There was no anointing present, no unction.

Pastor grabbed me by the hand and led me to other side of the room. He stood another couple before me, spoke more words in tongues over them, and then directed me—inaudibly, of course—to interpret.

Again, I crashed.

"Surely, he'll realize I don't have this gift," I silently prayed. "Tell him to find someone else to do this!"

But no. He led me to a third couple.

Shaking as I walked, I rehearsed the promise of 2 Timothy 1:7 (NKJV): "God hasn't given us a spirit of fear, but of power, love and self-discipline."

But that didn't help. I encountered the fourth couple—again, with no result.

Pastor Benny would not—even though he could see I was dying—allow me to return to my seat. He persisted, taking me to a fifth person.

Finally, about the sixth time he did this—and, I tell you, it felt like we had been doing this, treading water in the ocean of nothingness, for a long while—my flesh melted away. I was at the absolute end of myself, which is when the Holy Spirit stepped in.

Instantly, I prophesied. And, from that moment, I've always been able to do so. And in doing so, I've been able to breathe life and hope into others.

Paul speaks to this in 1 Corinthians 14:1-5 (NIV) as part of his lengthy passage on tongues and prophesy. He tells us:

> *Follow the way of love and eagerly desire gifts of the Spirit, especially prophecy. For anyone who speaks in a tongue does not speak to people but to God. Indeed, no one understands them; they utter mysteries by the Spirit. But the one who prophesies speaks to people for their strengthening, encouraging and comfort. Anyone who speaks in a tongue edifies themselves, but the one who prophesies edifies the church. I would like every one of you to speak in tongues, but I would rather have you prophesy. The one who prophesies is greater than the one who speaks in tongues, unless someone interprets, so that the church may be edified.*

Notice that others are *encouraged* when we boldly step out to prophesy. When we don't, when we settle into fear (as I did the first five or six times), people miss out on something God wants to gift them through us.

DIE TO SELF, LIVE IN SPIRIT

Later, I asked Doc why I couldn't do it and then suddenly could. He reminded me of how Kathryn Kuhlman's ministry profoundly affected him.

(For a season, to be near the move of God through her, he even sang in her choir. In fact, he met John Arnott, the leader of the Toronto Fire movement, in that same choir! She impacted both giants of revivalism.)

When "Ms. Kuhlman" died (Doc always referred to her as "Ms. Kuhlman as an address of honor), her team reached out to Pastor Benny: "We want you to minister at her memorial service."

They outlined the plan. Several people would speak. Then, they would show one of the only professionally recorded videos of Kathryn Kuhlman ministering at a crusade. They felt certain the recording would bolster people's faith, usher in the anointing, and create an environment in which the Holy Spirit would freely move.

"At this point," they said, "you'll just step out and begin ministering to people in the way you already know how to do."

Pastor agreed and was honored.

Just before the meeting a woman named Maggie, Ms. Kuhlman's personal assistant, found Pastor Benny to encourage him. "Don't go back to your hotel and spend hours and hours preparing for this meeting. Just come rested and relaxed. It's a big meeting, and it's important, so take it easy that day. Allow the Holy Spirit to do what He wants to do."

He later confessed to me, "That sounded like one of the most unspiritual bits of advice I'd ever heard. I went and prayed my heart out for 2 or 3 hours. I had to make sure I was right with God!"

When it was time for the meeting, he was tired. In fact, he missed his cue to walk onstage. The worship leader clearly communicated which song would be his last, but Doc froze behind the curtain.

The worship leader sang the song again, thinking he might catch the cue the second time through. He did, but he couldn't move. He stood backstage, frozen stiff.

So they led the crowd through the song another time. And then yet another.

One of the assistants pushed Pastor from behind the curtain and out onstage. He fumbled around, found his way to a microphone, and began singing . . . in the wrong key.

Now, if you've ever heard him sing, you know Pastor Benny has a fabulous voice. He's a wonderful worship leader. Not that day, though. In fact, the entire meeting began to take a nose-dive, just like that

Sunday evening worship service when Pastor forced me to interpret his messages in tongues.

"The problem," Doc told me, "was that I was so caught up in myself that I assumed I mattered—that the weight of this meeting and the move of God was on me. It wasn't, though. The gifts of the Spirit aren't earned, they're freely given, according to 1 Corinthians 12:7 (author paraphrase)."

"What did you do?" I asked him.

He told me, "I simply lifted my eyes and said to Jesus, 'I cannot do this.' And as soon as I said that, I heard Jesus respond, 'I'm so glad you realize that, because now I can!' Immediately, the presence of God fell, the atmosphere shifted, and many were touched and healed."

As he spoke these words to me, I remembered other truths from that same passage, realities like "There are different kinds of working, but in all of them and in everyone it is the same God at work" (1 Corinthians 12:6, NIV). And, "All these are the work of one and the same Spirit" (1 Corinthians 12:11a, NIV). In other words, God does the work—not us.

Or, to say it in Doc's words, "It isn't about your ability, it's about your availability."

WITH GOD, YOU CAN

Whether you stand to interpret or pray or preach or serve or minister or do any other thing on behalf of God, you're simply the vessel. He does the work through you, but it's only your responsibility to be available. He's the one supplying the Spirit.

This is what it means to co-labor with God. We work, but He does the work. And that means we must learn how He moves in our lives, which often takes practice.

Doc told me, "You'll never prophesy until you prophesy. You'll never pray for the sick and see them healed until you pray for the sick and see them healed. You'll never minister in any way until you actually minister in that way."

Many people are anxious about the gifts of the Spirit. They're timid. They're—as I was—afraid.

They're often nervous they'll "get it wrong." Or that they won't "have the gift."

Remember how I felt that Sunday night?

This stance seems somewhat odd, because we don't expect preachers to speak like Billy Graham or Peter at Pentecost the first time they speak. Nor do we expect worship leaders—men and women we affirm are called—to "get it right" the first time they lead.

In fact, we anticipate they'll need training and time and many opportunities to use their gift until they walk in the full maturity of it. We're not disappointed in them throughout the learning process.

"This is just part of it," we tell them.

We rightly encourage them, coaching them as they move forward. Sometimes, we invest thousands of dollars to send them to Bible college or seminary or even conferences where they can better hone those gifts.

Yet someone stands to deliver a word of prophecy and misses it, and we often assume, "Hmmm... they—or I—must not have the gift."

Can you imagine looking at a toddler who is learning to walk yet keeps tripping, then looking at them and declaring, "Walking must not be your gift. Maybe it's something else."

STEPPING OUT WITH HUMBLE CONFIDENCE

Acts 4:31 (NKJV) tells us that the disciples moved with boldness: "After they prayed, the place where they were meeting was shaken. And they were all filled with the Holy Spirit and spoke the word of God boldly."

That's the place we must go—to that space where we "put ourselves out there," knowing that the results all rest on God, not us.

One day, I stood beside Doc in a prayer line. He ministered to hundreds that evening. The prayers were all short—and strong.

"The power of the Holy Ghost goes through you!" he repeated, snapping his fingers with each declaration to each individual person who approached him for ministry.

"The power of the Holy Ghost goes through you!" he said again, snapping.

And yet again—a snap and then the declaration: "The power of the Holy Ghost goes through you!"

With each statement, something visible happened. The Spirit manifested upon the person in a tangible way we could all see.

After this occurred a few times, he looked back at me. "I'm going to teach you something," he said. "Watch closely."

When the next person in line approached him, he quietly whispered, "Holy Spirit, please touch this person."

Nothing.

No change.

No manifestation.

Doc asked, "Do you know what happened?"

I replied, "No, I can't tell . . . because that's the way most people pray—very calmly, in an easy voice."

"That's right," he said. "The Holy Ghost is *never* released through timidity. Only through boldness."

I didn't understand. He could tell.

"Watch," he continued. Then, he prayed again in that calm voice, "Holy Spirit, please touch this person."

Again, nothing.

Then, a third time, he prayed very gently, "Holy Spirit, touch this kind person..."

No change.

He repeated the revelation, "Mattox, the Holy Ghost is only released through boldness." He turned toward the person and declared, in the strong voice, "The power of the Holy Ghost goes through you!"

This time, the Spirit responded and touched the person!

> **HE SIMPLY NEEDS A WILLING VESSEL TO STEP FORTH, SOMEONE WHO REALIZES THAT THE SPIRITUAL POWERS ARE "ON HIM" YET THE PHYSICAL PRESENCE IS ALL "ON THEM."**

This was a powerful, memorable moment. I learned—rather, it was revealed to me—that boldness is the key to unlocking God's power. The enemy would love for us to tip-toe through life, wondering if and when God might want to touch someone—or if it's even His will that we minister to a person.

We don't see that happen in the Bible, though:

- Jesus declared that the leper was healed (author paraphrase, Matthew 8:3).
- Jesus verified that the centurion's servant was well (author paraphrase, Matthew 8:13).
- Jesus told the paralytic to take up his mat (author paraphrase, Matthew 9:6).
- Jesus prayed and then shouted for Lazarus to come forth (author paraphrase, John 11:43).
- Peter commanded the lame beggar to walk (author paraphrase, Acts 3:6).

Moreover, a quick read through the New Testament reveals many more examples of this same type of boldness. We tend to pause, step back, and wonder if God wants to touch someone, but the scriptural truth is that He desperately wants to reveal Himself in miraculous ways. He simply needs a willing vessel to step forth, someone who realizes that the spiritual powers are "on Him" yet the physical presence is all "on them."

SEEING THE UNSEEN—AND TAKING ACTION

Sometimes, we must fight against what we see in the natural when we're bold. In fact, we most often do.

Pastor taught me about the Word of Knowledge as it relates to this. The Word of Knowledge, which we read about in 1 Corinthians 12:8 often imparts facts and information about a person or situation to us so that we know God's heart for them—and it's delivered by the Holy Spirit in such a way that there's no natural explanation. Because of this, the person knows that God sees that and is for them, as He goes "out of His way" to tell someone else something about them they couldn't have known apart from God's intervention.

Because of this, the Word of Knowledge often carries faith with it—that is, the spoken words impart faith that God is actively moving and that something positive will happen. Remember, "faith comes by hearing—and hearing comes by the audible declaration of the Word of the Lord" (Romans 10:17, author paraphrase).

In one of our meetings, Pastor walked straight toward a woman in the crowd: "You have cancer," he said, "and the Lord is healing you right now."

"I don't have cancer," she contested.

He countered, "Don't lie to the Holy Ghost!"

I felt like those cartoons whose jaws drop and smash against the floor. I couldn't believe he said that—in front of everyone!

Whereas I would have likely apologized to the woman, Pastor Benny continued, "You do have cancer, and the Lord is healing it."

She began to sob. "You're right," she admitted. "I do have cancer. I've been taught not to confess it or say it out loud and agree with it. But I have it. I do have it."

"You need to know that the Lord is healing you—right now," he said.

Immediately, the power of God overcame her.

RESPONSIBLE FOR MAN, NOT TO MAN

Pastor Benny always acted boldly in those moments. Though some critics suggested he should tone it down a bit, he always knew that his primary responsibility was before God—and to be a connector to that person.

As well, he recognized that each of those moments were sacred, that we may never be back at the same place in that same way with that same person again. If they needed a touch from God, he felt responsible to do his part—to be available for God to move through him, to seize the open door.

One night we visited a church where he was invited to minister. That day, it was just Doc and me.

He walked to the platform to lead worship—as he often does. The congregation sang for a few moments until Pastor Benny stopped the service.

He turned to the organ player and declared, "Lady, you're the worst organist I've heard in my entire life!"

I thought, "What? This is harsh! Here's a woman who is actively using her gift." I didn't say anything, though, because I learned that Pastor Benny always saw something more—something from the Lord which gave him the confidence to act with boldness.

He turned to the crowd, "Is there anybody in this church who can play this organ?"

A man in a military uniform stood to his feet. He marched to the platform with all the order and decorum you might expect.

The jilted player stepped aside, and he slid smoothly across the bench. He began playing, the presence of God pushed its way into the room, and miracles began to flow.

I was still perplexed, trying to make sense of what happened. Yet I couldn't deny that something had, in fact, changed. The atmosphere of the entire room shifted completely.

After the service we met with the pastor we were ministering for. I pondered how he might navigate all of this after we left. After all, we were "in and out," but he would remain there for the long haul. He would be the one to handle any fallout from this.

"The lady who played the organ," he began, "has been under such a spirit. Until you called her out, she was controlling the organ. She wouldn't let anyone play and would only allow certain songs to be sung."

In a moment, God handled it.

And, for sure, He loves the woman. She's a daughter of His. But at the same time, the spirit that shackled the congregation needed to go, so true worship could be unlocked.

We often think boldness means standing against the world—and that the only sins we need to address are "out there." Remember that a slave girl followed Paul and Silas, declaring "These are servants of the Most High God" (Acts 16:17, NKJV).

Though the words were true, they were demonically driven. Just like the woman, Paul immediately cast the demon out.

BOLDNESS IS NOT JUST FOR A FEW

One evening, decades later, Beverly and I went to eat dinner after ministering in a church. We were in a small town and found a restaurant that had a salad bar—a lot like Shoney's used to have. We sat beside that bar.

It was slow that evening, so the manager served us. He was a gentle, pleasant man. We began talking.

"What do you do?" he asked. "What brings you to the area?"

"Well, I'm a preacher," I said. "We just finished a meeting down the street."

"That's interesting. I've traveled all over the world studying different religions," he replied. "My wife and I are not Christian."

"Yes, I am."

THE SPIRIT IMPARTS BOLDNESS

As he continued checking on us over the course of our meal, the conversation unfolded. I felt the same boldness swell within me which felt so common from many of the crusades.

Later, as I was at the salad bar, he walked up to refill one of the dishes.

"Look," I asked him, "do you mind if I pray for you? I would like to pray that if Jesus really is the Son of God that He would reveal Himself to you."

"I don't mind at all—please pray!" the manager said.

Get the picture. We're in a restaurant. It's not crowded—it's late. But the place is clearly open for business. There's no worship, no background music, and no organ. It's just us and this new friend.

I reached for his hands and began praying, "Lord, Jesus, please reveal yourself to this man."

Suddenly, it felt like a freight train burst through the wall! A spiritual train ran through my body, jolted that man, and knocked him out—slain in the Spirit!

Beverly was sitting in the booth with a friend of ours. They *both* fell out onto the floor!

In other words, it looked a lot like the altar call at a crusade, but we were in a restaurant. I tell you, I was shocked more than anyone.

A few moments later, the man stood, tears streaming down his face. It was a strong encounter with the Lord, but it was pleasant and tender.

"What was that?" he asked. "In all my searching I've never experienced anything like that."

I said, "That's the Holy Spirit bearing witness that Jesus is who He says He is."

Right then, the man kneeled and accepted Jesus as Lord. There was no sermon and no invitation—just the authentic overflow of a genuine encounter beside the salad bar.

> **I SAW THAT PEOPLE AREN'T REPELLED BY GOD'S PRESENCE AND POWER, THEY'RE HUNGRY FOR IT.**

We've seen encounters like that many times. For instance, Beverly and I went to Cracker Barrel for lunch one day. Our meal came, and we asked our waitress if there was anything we could pray about for her.

She had recently lost her husband and was in great distress, so we asked the Lord to touch her. The Lord instructed us to financially bless her and to release powerful words of prophecy over her. The more we spoke, the more the Lord revealed His heart and compassion for her. She began to weep as the Lord touched her on a deep level.

After a moment, she told us, "I'll be right back."

She returned with another waitress, a friend of hers dealing with a drug addiction. As we prayed for her, demons manifested and she was delivered.

Then, a few tables over, a complete stranger raised her hand. "Can we be next? Will you pray for us, too? We're not from around here. We've been traveling. We're estranged from our children and grandchildren."

I saw that people aren't repelled by God's presence and power, they're hungry for it. It's magnetic. When God's people walk with boldness, the Holy Spirit steps in and does things only He can do.

A BEACHHEAD TO WHAT'S POSSIBLE

I believe the boldness Pastor Benny demonstrated from the stage is meant not only to be expressed in pulpits and on platforms but also in offices and restaurants and shopping malls and ballparks and homes and every other place we find God's children. The Holy Spirit is—I believe—looking for willing people through whom He might express Himself, people who realize that the willingness of the Spirit and the empowerment of the Spirit isn't dependent upon anything other than the fact that God has determined to work through them.

Or, to say it another way, Pastor Benny's ministry shows us what's possible when we're willing to give God room to move. Moreover, in the same way, as an invading army takes a strategic piece of land and establishes a supply chain whereby other soldiers can follow behind and take territory more freely, Pastor Benny broke new ground that now shows us how to walk with a demonstration of God's goodness in tangible ways—anywhere and everywhere.

There are so many things people misunderstand about Pastor Benny.

Someone asked me, "Why does he blow on people?"

Another inquired, "Why did he pick up a microphone and blow through the sound system?"

There are two answers.

First, Jesus actually blew on the disciples and received the Holy Spirit (author paraphrase, John 20:22). We see Biblical precedent.

Second, early in his ministry, Pastor Benny would touch people. He laid hands on the sick—like Jesus said His followers would do (author paraphrase, Mark 16:15-20).

However, some people began accusing him: "You're pushing people over. That's why they fall. They're not slain in the Spirit."

Wanting to remove any doubts about God's presence and power, Pastor Benny made a decision to stop touching people. As I mentioned earlier, he began snapping his fingers and blowing. That's how those behaviors emerged.

To summarize it, though, he was bold. He was willing to put himself "out there," even if it meant being humiliated, so that someone might know—and experience—that Jesus is real, that God is for them. He was willing to do whatever it took—and will do whatever it takes—to see someone touched by the Holy Ghost.

CHAPTER 3

THE SPIRIT IMPARTS HUNGER

Impartation simply means this: Through relationship, God often takes one ability and transfers it to another in such a way that neither is diminished. Rather, each gift multiplies as they're shared with others.

We see an example of this when the Lord imparts the "spirit of Moses" to the leaders in Israel. Notice Numbers 11:16-17 (NIV):

The Lord said to Moses: 'Bring me seventy of Israel's elders who are known to you as leaders and officials among the people. Have them come to the tent of meeting, that they may stand there with you. I will come down and speak with you there, and I will take some of the power of the Spirit that is on you and put it on them. They will share the burden of the people with you so that you will not have to carry it alone.'

Many people are familiar with the impartation that passed from Moses to Joshua. The Bible tells us that "Joshua son of Nun was filled with the spirit of wisdom because Moses had laid his hands on him. So the Israelites listened to him and did what the Lord had commanded Moses" (Deuteronomy 34:9, NIV). Notice the cause-effect correlation: Joshua was filled (the effect) because Moses laid hands on him (the cause).

For this reason, Paul encouraged Timothy not to set anyone into a position of authority hastily because he could (and would) impart something tangible to them. He wrote in 1 Timothy 5:22 (NIV): "Do not be hasty in the laying on of hands, and do not share in the sins of others. Keep yourself pure."

One the most well-known examples of impartation occurs in the story of Elijah and Elisha. In 2 Kings 2:9-15 (NIV) we read of Elijah being taken to Heaven in a fiery chariot. Before He goes, though, he asks Elisha a question as they cross the Jordan river:

When they had crossed, Elijah said to Elisha, 'Tell me, what can I do for you before I am taken from you? Let me inherit a double portion of your spirit,' Elisha replied. 'You have asked a difficult thing,' Elijah said, 'yet if you see me when I am taken from you, it will be yours—otherwise, it will not.' As they were walking along and talking together, suddenly a chariot of fire and horses of fire appeared and separated the two of them, and Elijah went up to heaven in a whirlwind. Elisha saw this and cried out, 'My father! My father! The chariots and horsemen of Israel!' And Elisha saw him no more. Then he took hold of his garment and tore it in two. Elisha then picked up Elijah's cloak that had fallen from him and went back and stood on the bank of the Jordan. He took the cloak that had fallen from Elijah and struck the water with it. 'Where now is the Lord, the God of Elijah?' he asked. When he struck the water, it divided to the right and to the left, and he crossed over. The company of the prophets from Jericho, who were watching, said, 'The spirit of Elijah is resting on Elisha.'

Notably, after this encounter, Elisha replicated several of the miracles we see in the ministry of Elijah. For instance, both men resurrected a widow's son (Elijah in 1 Kings 17:22, Elisha in 2 Kings 4:34, author paraphrase). A close read through the Scripture reveals Elisha performed exactly twice as many (recorded) miracles as Elijah. In many of the instances, the miracles not only multiplied; they also intensified.

> **SOMETIMES, PEOPLE RECEIVE AN IMPARTATION JUST BY BEING PRESENT WHERE THE HOLY SPIRIT IS MOVING.**

The example of Elijah and Elisha is interesting, because we can read the stories of both men and see the replication in action. Elisha clearly performed miracles and walked in an empowerment without any formal education. Rather, the supernatural capacity was imparted—it was transferred through relationship.

That's what impartation accomplishes. It accelerates the learning curve—and even outpaces it—because God leverages the personal interaction to pass things down that would otherwise be impossible to grasp.

Moreover, this happens through relationship.

After Peter healed the lame beggar in Acts 3, the religious authorities sought to squelch their message. Notice what Luke writes about Peter and John in Acts 4:13 (NIV), specifically what the Sanhedrin notices: "When they saw the courage of Peter and John and realized that they were unschooled, ordinary men, they were astonished and they took note that these men had been with Jesus."

"Unschooled, ordinary men" infers they were not formally educated. They did not learn the Scriptures in a rabbinical school or a seminary.

It's not that God is against education. He's clearly not. When He chose a man to write about the depths of grace—and even about the spiritual gifts—He tapped Paul, the man who was "educated at the feet of Gamaliel," a noted rabbi of the day. Paul reminds everyone that he "studied under Gamaliel and was thoroughly trained in the law of our ancestors. I was just as zealous for God as any of you are today" (Acts 22:3, NIV).

But because Paul *and* the disciples had been with Jesus, they all received Jesus' impartation, regardless of education, according to Acts 4:13. That's what the religious leaders noticed. Through that relationship, supernatural capacity was imparted to them.

Notice, too, that Acts 4:13 says they were "courageous." Some translations substitute the word bold—the same concept we studied in chapter 3 Both the relationship and impartation are reasons for this boldness. Impartation also works by proximity.

Relationship is not the only way impartation occurs, however. Sometimes, people receive an impartation just by being present where the Holy Spirit is moving.

THE SPIRIT IMPARTS HUNGER

Look at what happens in Acts 5:15-16 (NIV):

... people brought the sick into the streets and laid them on beds and mats so that at least Peter's shadow might fall on some of them as he passed by. Crowds gathered also from the towns around Jerusalem, bringing their sick and those tormented by impure spirits, and all of them were healed.

I watched this happen multiple times during my time with Pastor Benny.

I used to frequent the hotel gyms we stayed at—I know, most hotel gyms are not impressive, but they all have treadmills. Running a few miles on them helped me maintain stamina for the traveling and long nights at the crusades.

One day I was running on the treadmill at an Atlanta hotel. We were preparing for a massive crusade in town. I began speaking to the man running next to me. Through his broken English, I learned he was from Buenos Aires, Argentina.

"What are you in town for?" I asked.

He forged his way through the language barrier and explained, "I'm here to see the evangelist Benny Hinn. I want to receive a portion of the anointing he carries, so I can take it back to Argentina."

"How did you choose this hotel?" I replied, jogging side-by-side in place on the treadmill.

"I just looked for a hotel," he answered. "This one sounded good, so I came here."

"What's your name?" I asked.

"Claudio," he replied. "Claudio Freidzon."

"Claudio, it's interesting that we're here running together," I said. "My name is Kent. You're not going to believe this, but I work with Pastor Benny. Why don't you ride to the meeting with me tonight? I'll get you in and make sure you're positioned to receive whatever God has for you."

Let me provide some perspective for what I'm about to share. Pastor Benny's meetings were large, and the "rooms" filled quickly. Overseas, it wasn't uncommon to see anywhere between 100,000 to 1 million people attend. In the US, he regularly filled coliseums and stadiums seating 30,000-40,000.

That's what Pastor Freidzon and I encountered when we arrived. There were no seats available on the main floor. Many times, people were turned away.

"I'll take you to the platform with me," I said, sensing it might facilitate a set-up for a divine moment.

Claudio responded, "Okay!"

I could see he was half-excited, half-nervous. We both knew God had something planned.

A few minutes later, the meeting began. Pastor Benny walked onstage and began worshipping. The Lord's presence increased in the area.

Then, Pastor Benny whirled around and asked, "Who is this man?"

I explained, "He's a pastor from Argentina. He traveled all the way here to encounter the Presence and take an impartation of the anointing back to his country."

Pastor removed his jacket, placed it on the man, and he fell out. God touched him. Claudio received what he came for.

Claudio returned home after the crusade and continued leading his church. Things were different, though. His ministry ballooned from a 700-person church to packing stadiums with 100,000-plus people, because he received an impartation of the Holy Spirit. He later wrote a book about this seemingly random meeting in a hotel, the bizarre manifestation onstage, and the ripple effect that occurred as a result.

He also returned the following month with ten more pastors, each of them hungry for a move of God. Moreover, they were willing to go anywhere to receive it.

Each time they came, they received something just by being in the place where the Presence of God manifested. In the same way people in the Bible were healed by stepping under Peter's shadow; these men were empowered by stepping under the spiritual shadow of Pastor Benny's ministry.

This continued.

By the third month, twelve more pastors joined Claudio at the crusade. In fact, he travelled back and forth to the US. every thirty days for the next half year just to be near the presence and power of God. In total, over one hundred pastors experienced God in a fresh way, and as a result, an entire country began transforming, showing that you never know the full scope of what might happen through an impartation.

Remember, impartation does not mean we "give something away" and no longer have it. Rather, impartation *multiplies* whatever is shared. Now, both people have it and the impartation onto others can continue.

NO RIVAL FOR A TOSSED JACKET

I know, some people hear stories like this and think, "Yeah, I get it. God can do something when we're in one place—like all those pastors attending those meetings. But what about the jacket that started it all? How does that work?"

The honest answer is that I don't know how it works. I just witnessed it working, and I know that I see it in the Bible. At some point in the meetings, Pastor Benny often felt an unction to use his jacket as a point of contact to mantle others and release the Holy Spirit. And it worked.

Luke, one of Paul's traveling companions who chronicled several of the missionary voyages, wrote in Acts 19:11-12 (NIV), "God did extraordinary miracles through Paul, so that even handkerchiefs and aprons that had touched him were taken to the sick, and their illnesses were cured and the evil spirits left them."

In the Old Testament we learn that Moses anointed Aaron into the priesthood and doused him with oil. He also clothed him with a uniform—vestments—specifically described by God (see Leviticus 8-12, paraphrase).

Interestingly enough, we don't see future priests anointed with oil. Rather, we see their vestments handed down, the anointing going with them.

Moses and Aaron were forbidden from entering the Promised Land because of the rock-striking incident (Numbers 20, paraphrase). When it came time for Aaron to die, the Lord instructed Moses to take the priestly outfit from him beforehand and dress Eleazar, Aaron's son, so that he might now fulfill the priestly duties (Numbers 20:28, author paraphrase).

Again, I don't know how that transference—that impartation—works. I just know that I've seen it happen.

There were a group of Russian pastors who were hungry for the presence and empowerment of the Holy Spirit. They served before the Berlin Wall came down. One of them received a (contraband) video of Pastor Benny teaching from his book *Good Morning, Holy Spirit*. They received an impartation through the video.

An elementary school teacher in our movement heard about this concept and realized that she sends papers and drawings and reports home with her students several times each week. She said:

I decided to begin laying hands on and praying over everything I sent. Many of those items were going to get stuck on refrigerators and other prominent places to honor the children's achievements. I could send those power-packed packages home, soaked in prayer, and believe God to do something in that household like Paul's handkerchiefs!

She realized that she was not only a teacher of kids, she was also a minster of the Gospel. She was placed there, by God, to shepherd entire families into His presence.

Furthermore, impartation was one of the tools in her arsenal of grace.

A man in our town used to sing rock-n-roll in bars before he become a pastor. He was high most of the times he performed.

His mother, a praying woman, asked him if she could begin cleaning his apartment, just to serve him. He agreed.

When she did, though, she swabbed the entire premises with anointing oil. She made his bed—the same bed in which he sinned—and laid hands on it as she prayed aloud. She wrote notes of encouragement and placed them on the same pillows where he would later rest his drunken head.

One evening, he stumbled into the home, slouched across the bed, and reclined on that pillow. Suddenly, the Spirit of God crashed upon him, and he sat upright. Completely and instantly sober, he accepted the call to preach.

That was 35 years ago.

The contradiction I often hear about impartation from well-intended Christians is that many have no problem believing that the enemy can transfer something evil to them. However, they're skeptical that the Savior can distribute something good and holy in the same way.

That is, we have no problem believing that wayward people can influence us in the wrong direction. We even say things like "show me your friends and I'll show you your future." Or, "your life is a result of the five people with whom you spend the most time."

> **WHY ARE WE MORE CONFIDENT IN THE ENEMY'S ABILITY TO DECEIVE THAN WE ARE JESUS' CAPACITY TO LEAD?**

We're cautious about going to certain places, as well. In fact, some believers refuse to minister in specific areas because they're "so dark." Perhaps we forget that the One in us truly is, as 1 John 4:4 (author paraphrase) declares, far greater than the one who is in the world.

We have no problem accepting that things—physical items—can impart darkness. Many of us are hesitant when we see an idol (or mask) hanging on a wall, we don't like voodoo dolls, and we shudder when we see drug paraphernalia.

Why are we more confident in the enemy's ability to deceive than we are Jesus' capacity to lead?

Jesus Himself actually addressed this. He tells us that if we want something from Him, that we should ask. When we do, we can expect to receive. He said in Luke 9:11-10 (NIV):

So I say to you: 'Ask and it will be given to you; seek and you will find; knock and the door will be opened to you. For everyone who asks receives; the one who seeks finds; and to the one who knocks, the door will be opened.'

He likely anticipated some degree of questioning from His hearers, because He clarifies two chapters later:

Which of you fathers, if your son asks for a fish, will give him a snake instead? Or if he asks for an egg, will give him a scorpion? If you then, though you are evil, know how to give good gifts to your children, how much more will your Father in heaven give the Holy Spirit to those who ask him!" —Luke 11:11-13 (NIV)

Yet Jesus promised they would not "receive" the enemy if they sought God. Quite the opposite, they could fully expect the Father to shower them with the Holy Spirit!

Paul encouraged the Corinthians to "Follow the way of love and eagerly desire gifts of the Spirit, especially prophecy" (1 Corinthians 14:1, NIV). Lust is actually a better English counterpart for "eagerly desire." That is, we're told to hunger and yearn and crave for the Presence.

Practically, we do this in a two-fold way.

First, we honor the person with the gift we want to receive. In fact, I have learned you can only receive to the measure that you honor the gift.

Yes, God's messengers all have flaws. In fact, the closer you are to them, the more you will see those imperfections (I'll share more about this when I talk about the power of submission).

There's only been one "perfect" anointed person, Jesus. Notably, Acts 11:26 (author paraphrase) tells us that the disciples—who originally referred to themselves as "disciples" or "followers of the way"—began to be called Christians in Antioch.

Outsiders gave them this name. Furthermore, it's quite revealing that they named Jesus' followers after His anointing and not His name. Most followers of a movement are named after the founder or the founder's framework of teaching.

Not so with Jesus' followers. They were named after His anointing. You see, *Christ* is the Greek derivative of the Hebrew *Messiah*, which means "anointed one." People in Antioch saw them walking with the same power as their leader, the same supernatural capacity that was handed down from one to another.

Sometimes the power transferred through relationship.

Sometimes the power multiplied through close proximity.

Sometimes the power moved through physical items—such as cloths and aprons.

But it was all the capacity of the perfect Kingdom moving through imperfect people, men and women who were available (and hungry) for the Presence.

Second, we go to the place the gift operates. Let me explain.

A friend in my city who pastors a Methodist church encountered the Holy Spirit and began walking in the realm of miracles.

One day I asked him, "What changed? How did this happen?"

He told me, "I looked back at my Methodist roots. John Wesley, the founder of Methodism, said that 'if you weren't in revival and wanted to be, you should go find one that's happening. Just get in the room and experience it there, allowing it to wash over you.'"

I would add this, too. If you're a businessperson and want to discover how to operate your company for the glory of God—and do so at the capacity of Heaven—learn from someone who is actively doing it. Honor them. Go to them. Receive an impartation.

If you're a new father and want to learn how to love and lead your family in such a way that your home exudes supernatural power, find someone who lives at that level now and go receive the impartation.

YOUR INVITATION TO RECEIVE

Consider this your invitation to receive.

    I wrote this book for a few reasons. First, I want to honor my pastor and spiritual father—a man I know personally.

    Second, I feel responsible to steward the revelations I received from him. My prayer is that you will take them, add to each of them, and pass them through multiple generations; that you will be blessed, your children will be blessed, and even your grandchildren will experience something unexplainable apart from, well . . . *impartation*.

    Can a book do that?

    I don't know. But I do know that God can.

CHAPTER 4

THE SPIRIT IMPARTS THE INEVITABILITY OF A PERSONAL RELATIONSHIP

Many of Doc's books were written on airplanes during the commute back and forth from Orlando to the monthly crusades. We didn't travel with fancy laptop computers. Back then, we created books on old school yellow notebook pads.

Many people know Pastor Benny because of his book *Good Morning, Holy Spirit*. I received the two-fold blessing of helping Doc pull the book together as well as watching the unfolding relationship he had with the Holy Spirit which formed the basis of the book. He interacted with the Holy Spirit in the same way you and I relate to our friends. It was intimate; it was a companionship.

He told me about a meeting he attended when Kathryn Kuhlman ministered. During the meeting, she sensed someone had grieved the Holy Spirit, and she began crying—much like we might do if someone hurt a close friend or family member.

"Please don't grieve Him," she pleaded. "He's all I've got."

Pastor Benny told me that, in that moment, something unlocked in him. He sensed that if the Holy Spirit really is our Helper—the One Jesus sent so that we wouldn't be alone—then the Spirit probably has a personality. The Spirit can relate, think, feel, sense delight, and even grieve.

A quick study of Scripture revealed this to be true.

Jesus rejoiced in the Holy Spirit (author paraphrase, Luke 10:21).

We're told not to put out the Spirit's fire (author paraphrase, 1 Thessalonians 5:19), which infers we can also "fan into the flame" (author paraphrase, 2 Timothy 1:6).

We don't have to worry about what we will say in a situation, because the Holy Spirit will speak through us (author paraphrase, Matthew 10:19-20).

The Spirit knows the mind of God and will share God's purposes with us (author paraphrase, 1 Corinthians 2:11).

And, yes, the Spirit can be grieved, just as Kathryn Kuhlman said that night in the worship service. For that reason, Paul encouraged us not to grieve the Holy Spirit (author paraphrase, Ephesians 4:30).

GOOD MORNING, HOLY SPIRIT

Pastor Benny's intimacy with the Holy Spirit goes back to the morning he woke up after traveling home from Kathryn Kuhlman's meeting.

When he was living with his parents, he found himself exhausted after that trip. He had been riding on a bus for long hours. He laid in his bed, sleeping soundly through the evening.

He awoke the next morning, and the words came from his mouth, "Good morning, Holy Spirit!"

In that moment, the Spirit of God entered his bedroom and made Himself known. The same intense presence he felt in the meeting was now on him in his bedroom. The glory, to use the language from the Old Testament, filled the place (author paraphrase, 2 Chronicles 7:1). This happened not only that first day, but it occurred every subsequent morning for over a year.

A few days earlier he had watched "Ms. Kuhlman," as he refers to her talk about her intimacy with the Holy Spirit. He now experienced it himself.

Pastor Benny's routine became:
- Wake up.
- Greet the Holy Spirit.
- The Holy Spirit makes His presence tangibly known.
- The two fellowship together for eight to ten hours.

Furthermore, the Holy Spirit taught Pastor during this time—just as Jesus promised in John 14:26 (NIV): "But the Advocate, the Holy Spirit, whom the Father will send in my name, will teach you all things and will remind you of everything I have said to you."

We read a similar statement in John 15:26-27 (NIV): "When the Advocate comes, whom I will send to you from the Father—the Spirit of truth who goes out from the Father—he will testify about me. And you also must testify, for you have been with me from the beginning."

During those days in his bedroom, the Holy Spirit visited with Pastor Benny and revealed the reality of Scriptures, as well as the character of Jesus. He didn't just learn stories and theological concepts—though he certainly did learn those things. More than that, He began to truly know God.

Pastor Benny learned to read the Scriptures during this time and pray simultaneously. Rather than approaching God with a list of his concerns, he began to truly recognize that God "knows what we need before we ask," as Jesus testified in the Sermon on the Mount (Matthew 6:8, NIV).

He often started by reading the Word. After all, the same Spirit we want to lead us in prayer is author of Scripture (author paraphrase, 2 Timothy 3:16-17). The Word and the Spirit, Doc taught, will align.

Often, in his reading, the Spirit would illuminate a specific verse or phrase, as if it say, "Here, this is where I want to take you today. Let's focus on this."

That quickening of the Spirit—perhaps you've felt it before—became one of the means in which the Lord led him through the Scripture.

The Bible tells us that God spoke to Moses, face-to-face, as a man speaks to another man (author paraphrase, Exodus 33:11). The same passage reminds us that even after Moses left the tent, Joshua remained and lingered. That's what Pastor Benny did. He lingered.

As a result, the Holy Spirit was incredibly comfortable with Pastor Benny, and Pastor Benny was extraordinarily trusting of the Spirit. I never saw him step onto the platform, tape a television program, or even lead a staff meeting without inviting the Holy Spirit into that moment and expressing his desire for the Spirit to orchestrate every moment. The miracles and manifestations we saw in public meetings were all evidence of this private relationship—and, dare I say it, deep friendship and camaraderie.

IF THE HOLY SPIRIT IS GOD…

This relationship touched every facet of Pastor Benny's life—in both big things and small ways. For instance, he told me about working at a mall kiosk when he lived in Toronto, Canada.

One evening, he left and found himself trudging through zero degree weather.

"It was the kind of cold that physically hurts," he said. "It was painful."

In a hurry to make his way home, he forgot his earmuffs. He wore a jacket and gloves, but his ears ached.

He thought about his friend, the Holy Spirit, and asked, "Is there something You can do about this to help me?"

Pastor Benny told me that, "I felt two hands come over my ears and cover them—and it was like they had hand-warmers on each of them. My ears became warm—and remained that way—until I got home."

Paul prayed for the church at Corinth, expressing his desire for them to find themselves pleasantly entangled in the Trinity. He decreed, "May the grace of the Lord Jesus Christ, and the love of God, and the fellowship of the Holy Spirit be with you all" (2 Corinthians 13:14, NIV).

The Bible tells us that God is love (author paraphrase, 1 John 4:8), and that God loved the world so much that He gave His Son (author paraphrase, John 3:16). We understand that Jesus embodied grace (author paraphrase, John 1:17). Notice that Paul—in the 2 Corinthians 13 verse—references the fellowship of the Spirit. This is God's desire for us. For Pastor Benny, the Holy Spirit wasn't just a theological concept to be understood but a person to be known—and enjoyed.

Throughout the Bible we see that the Holy Spirit is God, so the Spirit has the same characteristics as God. For instance, in the same way that God is everywhere (theologians use the word omnipresent to express this; that is, "all-present"), so also is the Spirit.

David expressed this truth in Psalm 139. He began by asking a rhetorical question, but then found himself wading through deep truths as he pondered the answer (139:7-12, NIV).

Where can I go from your Spirit? Where can I flee from your presence? If I go up to the heavens, you are there; if I make my bed in the depths, you are there. If I rise on the wings of the dawn, if I settle on the far side of the sea, even there your hand will guide me, your right hand will hold me fast. If I say, "Surely the darkness will hide me and the light become night around me," even the darkness will not be dark to you; the night will shine like the day, for darkness is as light to you.

To be clear, David suggested that if he journeyed to Heaven, he would find that the Holy Spirit was there. That makes complete sense. We would all agree.

He also determined that if he made his bed "in the depths"—some translations say Sheol, the place of the dead—the Spirit would already be there, as well. In addition, he would find this relational presence of God at every other place he might go.

Some of us carry misguided notions about the Holy Spirit. For instance, some Christians believe that the Holy Spirit has no interest in them until they're saved. Only then, they feel, does the Holy Spirit express interest in their lives.

Some people believe that God withdraws His presence from them when they sin, that He "plays the Hokey Pokey with them." They feel that "He's in" or "He's out" based on what they've done.

But David shows us the opposite is true. There's nowhere we can go from His presence. Nowhere.

When I look back at my story, I see that the Lord was with me every time I sinned in a drug house, as well as every time I "had it together" and acted morally upright. He was, as David declared, acquainted with all my ways (author paraphrase, Psalm 139:3).

Before we're saved, the Holy Spirit leads us to salvation. John captured Jesus' words about this in John 16:7-11 (NIV):

But very truly I tell you, it is for your good that I am going away. Unless I go away, the Advocate will not come to you; but if I go, I will send him to you. When he comes, he will prove the world to be in the wrong about sin and righteousness and judgment; about sin, because people do not believe in me; about righteousness, because I am going to the Father, where you can see me no longer; and about judgment, because the prince of this world now stands condemned.

Notice that the Holy Spirit will prove to the world incorrect about sin and righteousness and judgment (verse 8). The goal of this, of course, is that people who are walking in sin begin to believe about Jesus (verse 9), catch a glimpse of the right-standing He offers them with God (verse 10), and realize that the enemy has been judged—and that they can be free from his grasp (verse 11).

HE KNOWS ALL THINGS

My wife and I experienced this. We didn't have language for it until we walked with Pastor for a few years, but we both encountered the Holy Spirit before we ever knew the Lord.

Before we married, Beverly was a single mom and owned a catering company. She also worked full time as a bartender at an exclusive club in her town. Amid the craze of the late 70s and early 80s, she—then an opportunist—realized she could move some cocaine.

One evening, as she drove down the Eastern Seaboard with two kilos in the trunk, she experienced God. She saw the sky open. She explained it as if watching an old drive-in movie in the car—except the car was rolling.

As the Holy Spirit revealed an open vision of her with a man holding a microphone and preaching the Gospel to thousands of people, she chuckled and exclaimed, "You've got the wrong girl!"

Then God laughed. "We'll see about that," He replied.

In other words, she knew it was the Lord. And, she knew what He communicated.

We met two years later. I was a regular patron at the club where she worked, so we knew of each other but didn't yet really know one another.

We both happened to be there one night when she was off. We began talking, found ourselves in the middle of a wonderful conversation, and decided to go out for dinner. We smoked a little and drank a little. That's just what we did in those days.

After a few moments, she became completely sober. She gazed at me—as if she was looking into my soul and not just looking at me. "You're going to be a preacher," she said.

"You sure are beautiful," I replied, "but you've got to be one of the craziest chicks I've ever met. I am not going to be a preacher."

"No," she said. She seemed certain.

"No?"

"You will be. I saw you." She relayed the vision she received while driving her car that night, then continued, "You're that man in the vision. The Holy Spirit showed you to me."

From the moment Beverly spoke those words, my life came unglued. Everything began falling apart—emotionally, financially, and even physically. I overdosed three times and found myself recovering in the hospital. Yet, amid this chaos, the Holy Spirit began to take control of our lives.

We married soon after we met. The Holy Spirit led me to a church even before I was saved. The Holy Spirit visited Beverly in the car one night, just as she was about to smoke a joint. Before she could light it, He showed her who Jesus really is.

> **THE SPIRIT NOT ONLY IS EVERYWHERE, THE SPIRIT ALSO KNOWS ALL THINGS.**

It's good news that the Spirit is always near us. And I'm staggered by the absolute grace the Holy Ghost embodies.

The Bible promises that we will find Him when we seek Him (author paraphrase, Jeremiah 29:13). Here's why: because when we finally look up and acknowledge His presence, as Pastor Benny did, we realize He's been there all along. Moreover, we discover that the Holy Spirit is not only present at salvation (and after), but the Holy Spirit works in our lives at each moment even before salvation leading us to an awareness of His abundant grace.

The Spirit not only is everywhere, the Spirit also knows all things. Theologians refer to this as *omniscience* (*omni* = all, *science* = knowing).

Paul argued that none of us have the capacity to counsel God (as we often try to do!), because we don't know the mind of God. In Romans 11:34 (NIV) he asked the rhetorical question, "Who has known the mind of the Lord? Or who has been his counselor?"

Notably, there is One who knows the complete mind of God—the Holy Spirit. In 1 Corinthians 2:9-12 (NKJV) Paul reminds us:

However, as it is written:"What no eye has seen, what no ear has heard, and what no human mind has conceived"—the things God has prepared for those who love him—these are the things God has revealed to us by his Spirit. The Spirit searches all things, even the deep things of God. For who knows a person's thoughts except their own spirit within them? In the same way no one knows the thoughts of God except the Spirit of God. What we have received is not the spirit of the world, but the Spirit who is from God, so that we may understand what God has freely given us.

In the same way you know what you are thinking, so also does the Spirit know what God is thinking—because the Spirit is God (verse 11). Furthermore, God gives us full access to this same Spirit (verse 12).

I remember teaching this truth at the church one Sunday—that the Holy Spirit is God, so the Holy Spirit knows all things. Whereas we often limit what we think God knows (and cares about, in our mind) to spiritual things, leave it to new believers—people who don't have enough formal religion in them yet—to remind us that God doesn't just know "Bible" things, He knows absolutely everything.

> **THERE'S NO DOMAIN OF KNOWLEDGE IN WHICH THE HOLY SPIRIT PROVES IRRELEVANT.**

A young man in our church who'd just given his life to the Lord told me he was working in his field one day when the engine on the tractor locked up. He didn't know much about farm equipment but had been trying to prep his property for some work he wanted to do.

"I just sat there bumfuzzled for a moment," he said. "I mean, I had planned to do all of that work on this day, and there was no way I could do it by hand. I needed the tractor to run."

He remembered the teaching from the recent sermon, then pondered, "If God knows everything... and if the Holy Spirit is God... then the Holy Spirit must know everything... and if the Holy Spirit knows everything, then that means the Holy Spirit must know about tractors."

The young man prayed the most nonspiritual but heartfelt prayer he'd ever voiced. "Holy Spirit, I'm in a jam. Will you show me how to fix this tractor?"

The Spirit began speaking: "There, take that wire..." Then—"Make this connection." And—"Tighten that." As well as—"Now, go crank the engine."

"The Holy Spirit fixed my tractor!" he said. "I didn't have a manual, but I had the Creator and Sustainer of all things. And I really mean all things. Even farm equipment."

This means that the Holy Spirit can guide you towards a better marriage, the Holy Spirit can help you build your business, and the Holy

Spirit can help you manage your health. In other words, there's no domain of knowledge in which the Holy Spirit proves irrelevant.

THE VOICE WHO SPOKE THEN SPEAKS NOW

Pastor Benny taught me that the Holy Spirit reveals Himself more fully as we obey and act on the knowledge we have received. That is, after we act upon one of His directives, He offers us another layer of instruction.

Acts 5:32 (author paraphrase) actually says it clearly: God gives the Holy Spirit to those who obey Him.

I've experienced this unfolding encounter, this dynamic relationship with the Holy Spirit. You likely have, as well.

The first time the Holy Spirit ever spoke to me was during one of Pastor Benny's worship services, shortly after we arrived in the Orlando area. It happened during the offering, just as the plates were passed.

"Give $100."

It was a quiet voice within me, yet I knew it wasn't me. We didn't have that kind of money. In fact, we had just moved to town, almost destitute. We didn't have much more than that in our checking account.

I looked to my wife. "I think the Holy Spirit just spoke to me," I said.

"He did," she replied. "You're supposed to give $100."

We were elated. Both of us had heard Him. We were beginning to identify what He sounded like and understand His ways.

It didn't just happen in church services, though—or about things we might classify as "religious." For instance, I pushed a shopping cart full of groceries to my car one day, loaded them into the truck, and then shoved the buggy back towards the bin.

I jumped into my car to drive off and that same voice whispered, "Wait. You're not done. Take that buggy all the way back to where it came from."

I recognized Who it was. It was the same One who told me to give $100 to the church. Yet here He was outside the church, intervening in something so small that it might seem petty and irrelevant.

I tell you, whether it's an extended time of prayer when you awaken, cold ears, a stalled tractor, an offering at church, or something as seemingly insignificant as a shopping cart, the Holy Spirit wants to be involved.

PART TWO

ACTIVATING SPIRIT-LED IMPARTATION

CHAPTER 5

ACTIVATION THROUGH WORSHIP

In a previous chapter we talked about the Holy Spirit. One of the Holy Spirit's primary functions is to lead us to Jesus. The Spirit does this before we're saved, as well as after we're saved. He reveals Jesus to us (author paraphrase, John 16:14-15), seals us with salvation (author paraphrase, Ephesians 1:13), and baptizes us into the Body of Christ (author paraphrase, 1 Corinthians 12:13).

Ultimately, it's all about Jesus.

In John 7, Jesus visited the Temple for the Feast of Tabernacles. This was one of the three major feasts in Judaism, a time when everyone gathered to remember that God provided for the Children of Israel as they dwelled in tents during their forty-year roam through the wilderness.

On the final day of the festival, part of the festivities included pouring seven large vessels of water from atop the Temple stairs. The water would cascade down, emphasizing God's abundance and provision—even in the desert.

With this in view, John writes in John 7:37-39 (NIV):

On the last and greatest day of the festival, Jesus stood and said in a loud voice, "Let anyone who is thirsty come to me and drink. Whoever believes in me, as Scripture has said, rivers of living water will flow from within them." By this he meant the Spirit, whom those who believed in him were later to receive. Up to that time the Spirit had not been given, since Jesus had not yet been glorified.

Pastor Benny taught me two things about this passage.

First, he reminded me that John tells us that the abundance of water demonstrates what the Holy Spirit would be like in the life of a believer (verse 38). We spoke about this intimacy in a previous chapter.

Second, he pointed to the fact that Jesus provided this image before the Spirit was given to us, which didn't occur until after Jesus was fully glorified (verse 39).

Avid readers of Scripture might recall that Jesus pointed to the Cross as the "hour of His glory." In John 12:23 (NIV), He said, "The hour has come for the Son of Man to be glorified." After He rose from the dead, He blew on the disciples in the Upper Room and told them to "receive the Holy Spirit" (John 20:22, NIV).

After the Ascension, Jesus baptized the disciples in the Holy Spirit, something Peter declared was possible because it was yet another step toward His glorification. He said, "Exalted to the right hand of God, he has received from the Father the promised Holy Spirit and has poured out what you now see and hear" (Acts 2:33, NIV).

When we recognize that Jesus' transition from Earth to Heaven wasn't just a geographic move—like traveling from Galilee to Jerusalem might be—but was an additional step in His glorification, it makes all the more sense that the Spirit would come forth in greater power in Acts 2.

Remember what Paul wrote in Philippians 2:5-11 (NIV) in this familiar passage:

In your relationships with one another, have the same mindset as Christ Jesus: Who, being in very nature God, did not consider equality with God something to be used to his own advantage; rather, he made himself nothing by taking the very nature of a servant, being made in human likeness. And being found in appearance as a man, he humbled himself by becoming obedient to death—even death on a cross! Therefore God exalted him to the highest place and gave him the name that is above every name, that at the name of Jesus every knee should bow, in heaven and on earth and under the earth, and every tongue acknowledge that Jesus Christ is Lord, to the glory of God the Father.

Jesus' name is now elevated above every other name in the universe. To the degree that we acknowledge this—and celebrate it—the Holy Spirit, who comes to exalt Jesus, has more freedom to move among us!

In other words, Jesus is the key to the anointing. He is the Messiah (the word means "anointed"), and the Spirit flows more readily when the Anointed One is set in His proper place of honor.

WORSHIP CHANGES EVERYTHING

I've never met another man who loves Jesus as much as Pastor Benny. He has a passion for the Savior. He adores everything about Him—Jesus' Word, the Scriptures which reveal Him, Jesus' people, and Jesus' presence.

Many people know of Pastor Benny because of the fantastic moves of the Holy Spirit in his crusades. They don't know about private times he spent offstage kneeling before Jesus' throne. When he was young, he met a Methodist pastor who took several young men under his wing, discipling them in their walk with God. The pastor loved old hymns and imparted that to Pastor Benny. Sometimes, after our meetings, we stayed awake until three o'clock or four o'clock in the morning singing those same songs. Often, during those precious times, Doc told me, "If you will learn to worship Jesus, as well as seek to know and understand Him intimately, the Holy Spirit will help you in ways you can't imagine." The reason his meetings were so powerful is because of his private devotion to Jesus.

Many people know him as a preacher or faith healer, but at his core, Doc is a worship leader. He's actually the best worship leader I know, because he adores Jesus, he understands the ways of the Holy Spirit, and he desperately wants people to know and experience God.

WORSHIP BUILDS YOUR SAVINGS ACCOUNT

Pastor Benny used the analogy of banking to teach me how a private life of worship and study works.

"When you meet with the Lord on your own," he said, "that fills you. It's like a savings account which you build, over time, bit by bit. Every day you place a deposit into it." He explained that there's another part of your life that operates more like a checking account—"that's the part where you're studying to lead a class or preach a sermon. You deposit something in that you're going to spend fairly soon. It will be gone unless you replace it."

> **HE HAS MORE TO PULL FROM WHEN YOU HAVE A FULL ACCOUNT, SOMETHING THAT'S BEEN BUILT OVER TIME IN SOLITUDE WITH JESUS.**

I was reminded of that in real time. Often, when we left meetings I felt an adrenaline rush. We had just served in a powerful way.

At the same time, I could feel depleted and empty. I needed to rest. I need to restore my soul.

Pastor Benny told me:

Many pastors and leaders in ministry try to live off their checking account. You can't. You need the savings account. And you need to keep building it. There are going to be moments you're called to minister and you don't have time to go place anything in that checking account. If you have deep savings, though, you can always make a transfer.

I was reminded of multiple verses in the Scripture that tell us "do not worry about what to say or how to say it. At that time you will be given what to say, for it will not be you speaking, but the Spirit of your

Father speaking through you" (Matthew 10:19-20, NIV). For a season I had assumed this just meant "God will show up." Thankfully, He does. However, He has more to pull from when you have a full account, something that's been built over time in solitude with Jesus.

TRUE WORSHIP IS ALL IN

Pastor Benny taught quite often about the Tabernacle—and how the historical structure not only highlighted different facets of Jesus but how the path through the Tabernacle provides a roadmap for intimacy with Him. The seven main furnishings of the Tabernacle facilitate this fellowship.

The brazen altar is the first piece a worshipper would see in the Tabernacle (Exodus author paraphrase, 27:1-8, 38:1-17). This is where God cleared sin, so they could go further in the relationship. This was the starting point to walking in true spiritual depth—not the finish line. The brazen altar highlighted God's forgiveness and sacrifice—not our failures and shortcomings.

Pastor Benny taught that the sacrifice of praise is offered here.

The second item a worshipper in the Tabernacle met after the brazen altar was the bronze laver. Water was available to the priests, as well as to cleanse the sacrifice (author paraphrase, Exodus 29:4, 30:17-21, 38:8). Notice the progress. Worshippers moved from the sacrifice towards the throne room (the mercy seat, the ultimate goal). The washing along the way was an essential step.

Pastor Benny taught me that this refers to the washing of the water of the Word.

The third item in the Tabernacle was the golden lamp stand with the oils (author paraphrase, Exodus 25:31-40, 37:17-24). The light illuminated the path forward and represented the revelation of God's nature. The oils were painstakingly prepared, just like the principle of sowing and reaping—and were necessary for the process to work.

Pastor Benny taught me that this represents the illumination of the Holy Spirit.

The showbread was the fourth item in the Tabernacle progression (author paraphrase, Exodus 35:23-30, 37:10-16). Through it, God revealed who He is (Jesus is the bread of life and the Word to be consumed), as well as who His people were (twelve loaves represented the twelve tribes). Frankincense was also available on the same table, which represented worship. This is always our right response—intimate worship—to the revelation we see of God. Revelation about God and intimacy with God should work together.

Pastor Benny taught me that the bread of the presence points to Jesus, the Bread of Life (John 6:35).

The Altar of Incense was the fifth and next article of furniture in the Tabernacle (author paraphrase, Exodus 30:1-10, 37:25-28). Here, we see intercession and worship fused together in total harmony. This moves us beyond busyness. It moves us beyond the "stuff" of this world. We step into the true treasures of the Kingdom, with radical heart transformation (author paraphrase, Matthew 6:21). When the heart is pure, everything on the planet can be managed for godly purposes (author paraphrase, Titus 1:15, 1 Timothy 4:4-5).

Pastor Benny taught me that this is where we move from loud praise to intimate worship.

1) The Ark appears sixth in the Tabernacle (author paraphrase, Exodus 25:10-16, 37:1-5). The Ark contained three items:
2) The ten commandments, showing God's precepts and requirements

3) Manna, showing God's provision and His resources (even in the wilderness)

Aaron's rod that budded, showing God's people and relationships He places before us for our growth and our good.

Pastor Benny taught me that each of the items in the Ark represent our rebellion against God. However, the Ark is covered by the Mercy Seat.

The Mercy Seat is the final element of furniture in the Tabernacle (author paraphrase, Exodus 25:17-22, 37:6-9). The place where God met His people was the most intimate place in the tent. Like the seventh day, everything flows from this rest. Furthermore, this is a seat—denoting that people aren't running around and serving. The work has been done.

"God chose to meet us right on top of our rebellion," Doc told me. "He's there, because of the atonement."

The Mercy Seat is also the place from which God actively speaks, he taught. Revelation moves from here.

Notably, all of these elements point to Jesus. Furthermore, they draw us into deeper connection with Him. Indeed, as John declared, Jesus is "the way, the truth, and the life" (John 14:6, NIV). Furthermore, He takes us to the Father (author paraphrase, John 14:9-12).

WORSHIP CONQUERS THE FORCES AGAINST YOU

Again, true information about God flows from deep intimacy with God. Doc taught:

If you want to sense God's Spirit, then worship. Lift the name of Jesus. When you worship, you step into that realm. You approach move from the sacrifice—which is where so many people stop. You

ACTIVATION THROUGH WORSHIP

move beyond that to the other six revelations of God we see in the Tabernacle—His cleansing (laver), His presence through the written and Living Word and His people (bread), His illumination and insight (lamp stand), true connection and intimacy (incense), His abundant provision for everything we need (the Ark), and absolute peace (the Mercy Seat).

I remember two different encounters in which I experienced this—just as he taught. Furthermore, they were each unique and different.

The first occurred in the backseat of a car in a Walmart parking lot. I wasn't yet part of Pastor Benny's staff; I was just beginning to follow the Lord wholeheartedly.

During that season I was desperate. I felt as if I was surrounded by devils on every side—all trying to clamor back into the present from my past. Addictions. Fears. Phobias. Insecurities.

I couldn't shake them, but I discovered that each time I worshiped those enemies dissipated. So, during that season, I got into the backseat of my car—there was no one else there—and I began singing aloud the hymns and melodies I learned at Orlando Christian Center.

It worked so well that I repeated the process. The parking lot became my private sanctuary amid the hustle of working with my dad and volunteering in the church. I discovered—and I learned it from Pastor Benny—that at any time I chose I could step away from anything pressing against me and find the Lord's presence and peace.

The second encounter took place at a friend's house. Everyone had left the home, so I was alone.

I grabbed the remote to look for a game on TV when I heard the now familiar voice: "Why don't you just worship?"

> **IN THE SAME WAY NEGATIVE MUSIC SHIFTS OUR SPIRITS IN CERTAIN WAYS, THE SOUNDTRACK OF PRAISE ELEVATES US TO LIVE AT A HIGHER LEVEL.**

I set the remote aside and began singing from that chair in the living room. As I made my way through the first song, the glory continued growing stronger. Soon, His presence seemed to fill the whole house.

I sang a second song.

Caught in the moment, I sang a third.

As I finished the fourth, I thought, "I've never sensed anything like this before!"

Then, something occurred that marked me forever. The Lord Jesus asked me, "Will you sing me one more?"

His words reverberated through my spirit. I was moved that my worship touched my Savior so much that He asked for another song!

"I GOT BLESSED!"

It wasn't too long after that second encounter that I worshipped again in the same way. It was morning.

I saw an open vision in which Jesus stood from His throne and walked through Heaven. He greeted several of the patriarchs—Abraham and Isaac—and told them, "I just got blessed! Yes, that worship blessed me!"

I thought, "Lord, you're telling others that You were blessed—in the same way that we talk about getting blessed when we leave a worship service or meeting?"

The Spirit instantly took me to several verses throughout Scripture where I was shown that we have the capacity to bless God. He reminded me of the woman who anointed Jesus with the oil on His feet (author paraphrase, Luke 7:36-50). He reminded me of Palm Sunday when people shouted blessings over Jesus as He rode the donkey through the streets of Jerusalem (author paraphrase, Mark 11:1-11).

And then He showed me Psalm 103:1-5 (NKJV):

Bless the Lord, O my soul; And all that is within me, bless His holy name! Bless the Lord, O my soul, And forget not all His benefits: Who forgives all your iniquities, Who heals all your diseases, Who redeems your life from destruction, Who crowns you with lovingkindness and tender mercies, Who satisfies your mouth with good things, So that your youth is renewed like the eagle's.

Notice that, yes, we can bless the Lord (verse 1). Moreover, the benefits we're encouraged to remember all flow from that blessing, from the place of worship (verse 2).

For this reason, Pastor Benny always endeavored to make Jesus big. To use the "church word," he sought to magnify Him.

Create an atmosphere of worship. In the same way negative music shifts our spirits in certain ways, the soundtrack of praise elevates us to live at a higher level. Play worship music in your car. Sing melodies of praise as you rock your children to sleep.

Hebrews 13:15 encourages us to always "bring" the sacrifice of praise. We don't go to church to "get worship." It is something we take with us—everywhere we go. That way, we can emphasize the grandeur of Jesus over all things at all times.

CHAPTER 6

ACTIVATION THROUGH SUBMISSION

There's a phrase in ancient Hebraic culture which declares, "May you be covered in the dust of your rabbi."

Here's where it comes from. When someone was considered a renowned teacher, it was a great honor to be invited to become a student of that rabbi. Many young men in Israel wanted to become teachers.

So, when they were chosen by rabbis to follow (the rabbis actually selected their own students), they wanted to follow so closely that when the rabbi walked, the dust under their feet would kick back upon them.

It was their practice to follow and serve under the mentorship of another person, so that they could find their way into their own purpose and destiny. In our culture, unfortunately, we don't see this attitude of submission and following. It seems like everyone wants to lead immediately.

However, there's an art to following—and truths we learn through submission that make us better leaders. If we learn the practice of submission, we emerge exponentially stronger and more empowered to fulfill the call God places on us.

SUBMITTING TO GOD INVOLVES PEOPLE

The Bible instructs us to submit. Furthermore, we're promised that when we submit to God, we find safety and refuge. The devil runs away. James 4:7 (NIV) tell us clearly, "Submit yourselves, then, to God. Resist the devil, and he will flee from you."

Most of us think nothing about submitting to God. However, we often wince at what submission practically looks like.

Submitting to God includes deferring to the precepts we find in His written Word. Even when we don't understand the Scripture, our default stance is "God must know what He's talking about." Or, we disobey enough times and reap the consequences to realize the beauty of submitting to the Word.

There's another facet of submission, however. True submission also includes deferring to humans—to the people whom God places in our lives in specific roles.

Notice what we read about submission in Hebrews 13:17 (NIV) about submitting to spiritual leaders: "Have confidence in your leaders and submit to their authority, because they keep watch over you as those who must give an account. Do this so that their work will be a joy, not a burden, for that would be of no benefit to you."

ACTIVATION THROUGH SUBMISSION

In this verse, we're told not only to submit to our spiritual leaders. We're encouraged to have confidence in our submission. Furthermore, this makes their work on our behalf joyful and it benefits us.

When writing about marriage, Paul tells husbands and wives to "Submit to one another out of reverence for Christ" (Ephesians 5:21, NIV). The women are specifically instructed that this submission takes the form of respect; the men are instructed that their submission manifests as loving their wives in the same self-sacrificial way that Christ loves the Church, His bride.

The New Testament continues fleshing-out this concept of submission into other domains of life. For instance, Colossians 3:22-24 (NIV) applies this approach to the workplace:

Slaves, obey your earthly masters in everything; and do it, not only when their eye is on you and to curry their favor, but with sincerity of heart and reverence for the Lord. Whatever you do, work at it with all your heart, as working for the Lord, not for human masters, since you know that you will receive an inheritance from the Lord as a reward. It is the Lord Christ you are serving.

To be clear, the slavery to which Paul referred is radically different than the slavery we experienced in the United States. In his culture, people voluntarily indentured themselves to work for another person for a period of years. It could have been to pay a debt or even to earn a reward—such as when Jacob worked for Laban for seven years twice for a daughter's hand in marriage (author paraphrase, Genesis 29:17).

Don't miss the clear lessons expressed in this passage.

Submission involves the heart—not just doing the right thing when someone is watching.

Submission is work we do for the Lord—not the human who serves as the intermediary in that position.

Submission connects us to our inheritance—and the Lord will, in time, pay.

There's a power that comes from submission. We acquire lessons here (often the lessons are about ourselves!) which can't be gained any other way. The hardest part of submitting, though, is that submission—whether in a church or ministry, a family, or even the workplace—always includes other humans.

SPIRITUAL SUBMISSION

In this chapter, I want to focus on spiritual submission. I mentioned the other examples above, though, because I want you to see that this approach affects every area of life. Most people don't feel called to work "full time" in ministry. However, the same principles still apply. We still interact—and glean—from spiritual leaders, we all relate to families in some way, and most of us interact with employers.

Think back to the chapter on impartation for a moment. There, we learned that God uses people to connect other people to His presence and His provision. Though this can happen anytime people connect for Kingdom purposes, it happens in an exponentially elevated manner when a leader and follower walk in dynamic, intentional relationship.

Moses and Joshua walked together for over forty years. Joshua then walked in a new level of authority and helped the Children of Israel take their inheritance.

Elijah and Elisha spent years together. Elisha asked for a double-portion of Elijah's anointing and received it. In their story we see exactly twice as many miracles recorded.

Jesus and disciples journey together for over 3 years. He suggested they would do greater works than He did (John 14:12). In time, they turned the world upside-down (Acts 17:6).

Paul worked with Timothy. Much of the pastoral wisdom we read today is contained in the letters of lessons he shared with his young protégé.

Peter took Mark under his wing, according to history. Though Mark didn't personally walk with Jesus like Peter, he accumulated the wisdom and anointing of Peter. In turn, he penned the first biography of Jesus that was published. Furthermore, Matthew and Luke both used his outline as source material for their books.

When you walk under another, you serve their vision, their call. In fact, until you're released from them, that is your call—to undergird theirs.

WHY YOU'RE THERE

Because you walk closely with them, you see everything about them. You see their greatest attributes. You see their weakness, as well.

After the flood, Noah planted a vineyard. In time, when he harvested the grapes, he made wine. When he drank the wine, he became drunk.

His sons saw a man who heard God clearly and exhibited faith strong enough to invest decades constructing an ark in the middle of dry land for a pending flood—even though it had never rained. At the same time, they also saw a man who . . . well, acted intoxicated.

Notice how they responded differently to seeing the human side of him, however in Genesis 9:20-27 (NIV):

Noah, a man of the soil, proceeded to plant a vineyard. When he drank some of its wine, he became drunk and lay uncovered inside

> his tent. Ham, the father of Canaan, saw his father naked and told his two brothers outside. But Shem and Japheth took a garment and laid it across their shoulders; then they walked in backward and covered their father's naked body. Their faces were turned the other way so that they would not see their father naked. When Noah awoke from his wine and found out what his youngest son had done to him, he said, "Cursed be Canaan! The lowest of slaves will he be to his brothers." He also said, "Praise be to the Lord, the God of Shem! May Canaan be the slave of Shem. May God extend Japheth's territory; may Japheth live in the tents of Shem, and may Canaan be the slave of Japheth."

Clearly, one of the sons drew attention to Noah's imperfections (verse 22). The others covered those imperfections (verse 23). As a result, one found himself cursed; the other two received blessing.

In the same way, God "perfects you" by seeing human imperfections while simultaneously expanding your horizon to His supernatural operation through that person. You need both, because it creates the perfect synergy or radical humility (we're all human) and supernatural empowerment (God isn't human).

The Biblical word for perfect doesn't mean "without flaw," as we often suggest in English. The Greek correlation, *telios*, infers "to live up to its full potential." Or, "to fulfill the purpose for which it was designed."

Whenever I questioned something Pastor Benny did—something he might say, a decision he made, or how he handled a situation—the Lord clearly reminded me: "I didn't bring you here because of his strengths. He doesn't need you in those areas. I brought you here because of his weaknesses."

And when I mention *weakness* I'm not talking about sin, I'm talking about humanity. We all have areas in which we excel and areas in which we don't. We need each other, which is why God brings us together.

> **WHEN YOU WALK IN SUBMISSION, YOU'RE ACTUALLY MORE FREE TO LEARN.**

To this end, not only did I learn that his weaker areas were the places he actually needed my help the most, his areas of strength were the areas I needed training the most! That is, God not only led me to Pastor Benny so that I could serve him; he also led me to Pastor Benny because—even though it took years of experience of the wisdom of age to see it—Pastor profoundly served me!

Many of the lessons and revelations—I've shared in this book may have been the opposite of what you might have thought before reading the stories. Each of these revelations, however, are truths I acquired from Doc.

And, yes, some of the stories reference sermons or church meetings. Most of the lessons I learned, however, came not from large group gatherings, but from the quiet moments together. In other words, the best lessons emerge from relationship.

When you walk in submission, you're actually more free to learn. Part of the beauty of submission is that you don't carry the weight of the ministry. You're not the primary person responsible for leading and making—and then owning—the big decisions. You don't determine the outcomes; you do what you're told. This brings a safety and freedom—especially when you remember the three observations we made a few pages ago from Colossians 3:22-24.

HONOR YOUR MOTHERS AND FATHERS

In our culture, we've almost lost the concept of spiritual fathering and spiritual mothering. Those are the other sides of submission. If someone plans to submit, they must have someone to whom they can submit, someone the Lord will use to lead them.

Paul references this dynamic in 1 Corinthians 4:15. He tells the Corinthians that they have many teachers, but they don't have many fathers. This very much describes our society—even the church—today. We're inundated with information. We can watch the best preaching at any moment. We need only search YouTube, scan the podcast feeds, or swipe through social media. However, not many of us relate to others generationally, specifically for spiritual maturation.

In another passage, Paul encourages Timothy to continue forming others in the same way Paul helped develop him. In 2 Timothy 2:2 (NIV), he says: "And the things you have heard me say in the presence of many witnesses entrust to reliable people who will also be qualified to teach others."

Here, we see a baton passing. In the same way relay runners must work closely together—you can't toss a baton from afar—so also must we walk closely with others to ensure that information, revelation, and anointing (all of them!) continue getting passed. Not only do we not want to drop the exchange, we want to increase the intensity with each pass.

ACTIVATION THROUGH SUBMISSION

The Lord taught me a powerful lesson about this one day when I received a call from a church. About halfway into my decade with Doc, I felt like I was ready to preach.

The church—a large one—was looking for a pastor. They reached out to me, offering a healthy salary, an expense account, housing, and benefits to come and lead them.

"This must be the Lord!" I thought. "Holy Spirit, you're promoting me!"

As soon as I hung up the phone, the Holy Spirit replied, "Did Pastor Benny tell you to go?"

"No, he didn't..."

"Right now you're submitted to him, and you're serving him. That's your call during this season. If this church was the right move for you, I would have told Doc."

In hindsight, I'm so grateful, because my life would look totally different now had I taken that call and diverted my attention from God's intentions for me. I would have missed so many blessings and so much of the protection the Lord has sent my way by walking with a heart of submission.

Lest we think this is limited to pastors and ministers, the New Testament reminds us that this exchange often looks like everyday life. Titus, another of Paul's sons in the faith, was told to instruct seasoned women to lead their less experienced counterparts before receiving similar instructions about men (Titus 2:3-8):

> Likewise, teach the older women to be reverent in the way they live, not to be slanderers or addicted to much wine, but to teach what is good. Then they can urge the younger women to love their husbands and children, to be self-controlled and pure, to be busy at home, to be kind, and to be subject to their husbands, so that no

one will malign the word of God. Similarly, encourage the young men to be self-controlled. In everything set them an example by doing what is good. In your teaching show integrity, seriousness and soundness of speech that cannot be condemned, so that those who oppose you may be ashamed because they have nothing bad to say about us.

I wonder how things might be different if we focused more on these types of relationships.

After providing four commandments that denoted how Israel should relate to God, He provided six more that affirmed how they should relate to each other. The first of these, the fifth commandment, is found in Exodus 20:12 (NIV): "Honor your father and your mother, so that you may live long in the land the Lord your God is giving you."

The New Testament highlights this command as the first that carries a promise (Ephesians 6:1-3, NIV): "Children, obey your parents in the Lord, for this is right. Honor your father and mother"—which is the first commandment with a promise—"so that it may go well with you and that you may enjoy long life on the earth."

Now, notice the next verse (6:4, NIV): "Fathers, do not exasperate your children; instead, bring them up in the training and instruction of the Lord."

Though referring to household fathers, I think this passage applies to spiritual fathers as well. Both types of fathers are exhorted not to exasperate the people who are submitted to their leadership—that is, to literally "suck the wind out of them." It's easy to do—we can say the wrong things, we can use the wrong tone. Rather, we're told to breathe life into them, to blow wind into their sails so they can go farther, faster—so they can bypass our failures and shortcut our successes.

> **SUBMISSION ALLOWS US TO BENEFIT FROM THE EXPERIENCE OF ANOTHER. IN ADDITION, WE BENEFIT FROM THE EXPERIENCE OF EVERYONE THEY BENEFITED FROM.**

One day the Lord told me something related to this. He said there are two ways you can acquire the lessons you need to know in order to lead: "You can gain them by revelation or you can learn them by tribulation."

Yes, we can go through life on our own. Many people choose to do that.

"Let me figure it out," they say. And—"Even if I mess up, I want to mess up on my own."

Face it. Experience is a good teacher. But personal experience costs you one of your most valuable assets—time.

Submission allows us to benefit from the experience of another. In addition, we benefit from the experience of everyone they benefited from.

You reap not only from the time you sowed into their ministry, but from the time they sowed into their ministry. You stand on their shoulders.

Furthermore, remember that they reaped not only from the time they served in another's ministry, but they reaped from the time that person sowed in the ministry as well. In this way, we each stand upon one another's shoulders, elevating a generation of spiritual heirs to build upon the previous experience, revelation, and anointing.

JESUS SAW IT AND COMMENDED IT

Matthew tells of an encounter in which Jesus taught about authority and submission. One day, a centurion approached them (Matthew 8:6-10, NIV):

> "Lord," he said, "my servant lies at home paralyzed, suffering terribly." Jesus said to him, "Shall I come and heal him?" The centurion replied, "Lord, I do not deserve to have you come under my roof. But just say the word, and my servant will be healed. For I myself am a man under authority, with soldiers under me. I tell this one, 'Go,' and he goes; and that one, 'Come,' and he comes. I say to my servant, 'Do this,' and he does it." When Jesus heard this, he was amazed and said to those following him, "Truly I tell you, I have not found anyone in Israel with such great faith."

Notice that Jesus marveled at the man's great faith. It's in the final sentence of the passage.

Furthermore, the centurion saw that even Jesus lived under authority. That was the basis of His anointing, in fact. In the same way soldiers obeyed the commander because he was backed by the authority of Rome, demons and sickness and storms and everything else obeyed Jesus because of the authority of the Kingdom that backed Him.

It takes great faith to submit your life to a man or a woman, trusting that God will use a human being with their own weaknesses, to actually bring about the purposes of God in your life.

Yes, people can abuse authority. They can also abuse sex, money, and fire. Yet, we still enjoy the gift of intimacy and oneness, we leverage financial resources for our good and the benefit of the Kingdom of God, and when we eat a cooked meal in a warm home we enjoy the benefits that fire provides.

Don't miss the blessings—the increased revelation and anointing—available through submission.

CHAPTER 7

ACTIVATION THROUGH GENEROSITY

I decided to write this book for a few reasons.

First, Scripture encourages us to "give honor where honor is due" (Romans 13:7, NKJV).

Second, I was, as they say, "in the room where it happened." In the same way Luke wrote an orderly account of the things he—as an eyewitness—saw, so also am I (author paraphrase, Luke 1:2).

Third, I recall specific revelations I received from Pastor Benny which—unless I share them—might not be handed to others. Paul encouraged Timothy to pass "the things he received" to other faithful leaders who might do the same (2 Timothy 2:2, NKJV).

All that said, here's the truth: many people who weren't there often paint a portrait that's not necessarily true. Some do this out of spite, of course. Others do this simply because they have limited information.

Somebody once asked me about flying in private planes and different aspects of that lifestyle—and why a minister would do that and live like that. It's a fair question. But, without the complete picture, your view is skewed.

Here's the truth.

Many weeks we moved teams of forty to fifty people in order to run a crusade. We did so on a tight schedule, flying out of town and then zooming back to make it to lead our home church. It was cheaper and more efficient to manage our own timeline than to wait on the airlines.

Then there were the death threats. Many people didn't like the message Pastor Benny shared. They proposed to stop him at all costs. Sometimes, it was safer.

The fact is that Doc is one of the most generous people I know—if not *the* most generous. He walked through life with an innocence that God will provide everything he needs, regardless of the circumstances. He exemplified the promise of 2 Corinthians 9:8 (NIV): "And God is able to bless you abundantly, so that in all things at all times, having all that you need, you will abound in every good work."

RELEASE AND RECEIVE

I learned this from him: when we live with open hands, we're free to give and receive. When our hands remained closed, clinching onto whatever we possess, we're not open to receiving, and we can still lose whatever we're clinging to. He believed that as long as you didn't get "sticky hands" God could freely move resources through you.

I watched him sell all his jewelry, give away all the clothes in his closet, and empty the ministry coffers in order to build an orphanage or direct the resources to another need the Lord pinpointed to him. This happened multiple times.

I still find myself caught in the wake of Pastor Benny's generosity even today—over thirty years after working on his staff. Last year, Beverly and I traveled to Scotland to see some friends in ministry. While preaching at a church, a middle-aged woman approached us.

"I know you used to serve with Pastor Benny," she said. "My parents were acquaintances of Pastor Benny's and Suzanne's."

Here stood a person—an ocean away from Orlando—who was also acquainted with Pastor Benny. We exchanged a few pleasantries, made a few relational connections, and swapped stories.

"That was a great season," I told her. "I loved working with him. He was one of the kindest, most generous people I know."

After that she told me, "I agree. You probably don't know this. In fact, I don't think anyone does. My parents were tight financially and couldn't afford to send me to college. Pastor Benny found out about this and actually paid my tuition. All of it!"

"Really?!"

"It wasn't his ministry that did it," she said. She wanted me to know, "He did it himself."

"Well, I'm not surprised," I replied. "I meet people everywhere—still today—whom he blessed in some way, just like that."

Proverbs 11:24 (NIV) tells us that "One person gives freely, yet gains even more; another withholds unduly, but comes to poverty."

Sometimes, I wonder if Pastor continued gaining because he gave so much away.

Proverbs 11:25 (NIV) continues, "A generous person will prosper; whoever refreshes others will be refreshed."

He consistently saw beyond any scarcity that might exist and leaned into the abundance of the Spirit, expressing the character of the God who loved the world so much that He gave His only begotten Son (author paraphrase, John 3:16).

GIVE FOR RIGHTEOUSNESS SAKE

Over 2,600 verses in the Bible link generosity and righteousness. That is, you can't have one without the other: to live righteously is to live generously; to walk in generosity is to express righteousness.

> **JESUS SAID OUR HEART ACTUALLY FOLLOWS OUR TREASURE. WE GENERALLY BELIEVE THE OPPOSITE—THAT WE GIVE OR SPEND THINGS WE HAVE A "HEART" FOR.**

To put this in perspective, Jesus Himself talked about money more than Heaven and hell. Our relationship to resources affects every area of life.

Jesus presented money—not the devil—as the chief rival of our allegiance to God (see Matthew 6:24 (NKJV): "No one can serve two masters; for either he will hate the one and love the other, or else he will be loyal to the one and despise the other. You cannot serve God and mammon."

Jesus said our heart actually follows our treasure. We generally believe the opposite—that we give or spend things we have a "heart" for. Jesus contends the flow works in the reverse direction in Matthew 6:21 (NKJV): "For where your treasure is, there your heart will be also."

Jesus suggested that money (and the desire for things) was one of the three main issues people faced in being fruitful in their walk. The other two were the devil himself and lack of spiritual depth, illustrated in Mark 4:18-19 (NKJV): "Now these are the ones sown among thorns; they are the ones who hear the word, and the cares of this world, the deceitfulness of riches, and the desires for other things entering in choke the word, and it becomes unfruitful.

Later in the New Testament we read that the love of money is the root cause of many kinds of (though not all) evil. Notably, money itself isn't evil—the desire for it is, as 1 Timothy 6:10 (NKJV) outlines: "For the love of money is a root of all kinds of evil, for which some have strayed from the faith in their greediness, and pierced themselves through with many sorrows."

As such, repentance in the Bible often manifests itself in how people responded with their money. Here are two examples.

First, in Luke 3:10-14 (ESV), when John the Baptist was asked by various groups what they should to do outwardly to demonstrate their internal heart transformation, all three answers had to do with money or resources:

And the crowds asked him, "What then shall we do?" And he answered them, "Whoever has two tunics is to share with him who has none, and whoever has food is to do likewise." Tax collectors also came to be baptized and said to him, "Teacher, what shall we do?" And he said to them, "Collect no more than you are authorized to do." Soldiers also asked him, "And we, what shall we do?" And he said to them, "Do not extort money from anyone by threats or by false accusation, and be content with your wages."

Second, though not required to do so by Jesus, Zacchaeus responded with the grace of giving at his conversion in Luke 19:8 (NKJV): "Then Zacchaeus stood and said to the Lord, "Look, Lord, I give half of my goods to the poor; and if I have taken anything from anyone by false accusation, I restore fourfold."

Ultimately, we discover that money is merely a test—if we can use financial resources in a Godly way then we show that we can be trusted with the true riches of the Kingdom. Luke 16:11-12 (NIV) says, "So if you have not been trustworthy in handling worldly wealth, who will trust you with true riches? And if you have not been trustworthy with someone else's property, who will give you property of your own?"

This final point—about money being a test—proves interesting on several levels. Notably, this passage is about a dishonest manager. He acted unfaithfully with his master's possessions, so he was fired. In turn, he began cancelling the debts of people who owed that master money so he would have a place to go.

Jesus said, "The master commended the dishonest manager because he had acted shrewdly. For the people of this world are more shrewd in dealing with their own kind than are the people of the light" (Luke 16:8, NIV).

Then, He placed money—all resources, in fact—in the proper place. Rather than hoarding them, we should use them to help others. Specifically, we should leverage them for the purposes of the Kingdom, so that people connect with their Creator. In the same passage, Jesus told His disciples, "I tell you, use worldly wealth to gain friends for yourselves, so that when it is gone, you will be welcomed into eternal dwellings" (Luke 16:9, NIV).

WHEN GIVING GETS HARD

I learned to hold money loosely. Somehow, it's easier to do so when you don't have any than when you have a lot. That is, abundance may be a greater test than poverty!

Shortly after moving to Orlando, I found myself in debt. I was turning my life around, and I wanted to make sure every area fell under the Lordship of Jesus. I hadn't filed a tax return in years, and I knew this was an area I needed to get right.

I completed the required tax returns for the years I skipped and called them.

A pleasant woman greeted me, and then said, "No problem. You've got it all together now. You can just send a check."

"I don't have $25,000 sitting around." That's how much I owed them—$25,000. I asked, "Is there something else I can do?"

After a moment, the representative on the other end of the line told me, "We'll send someone to see you."

Gasp.

I quietly prayed, "You didn't deliver me from my addiction and save me to send me to jail for tax evasion, God." Then, another thought occurred: "Maybe you've called me to preach in prison."

I sat in that mental space for three days. At some point, someone told me, "No, you're trying to make it right. You don't go to prison for failing to file, you go to prison for fraud. You're just going to get penalized."

And "get penalized" I did. The IRS rep agreed to garnish my wages. I provided them a budget—the bare minimum we could afford to live on. They took the rest. Plus, they tacked a hefty interest rate to the unpaid portion.

Amid this, Pastor taught on tithing.

"This doesn't make sense in the natural," I told Beverly. "I mean, we've got this debt lingering over us—and we don't make that much anyway. Now we're supposed to give away 10%?!"

We both agreed, though, that we were supposed to do it—even if the math didn't work. For the next five years, we faithfully tithed and paid the debt to the U.S. Treasury.

But we discovered a massive problem: the penalties and interest continued accumulating as long as any outstanding taxes were owed. In those sixty months of scraping by the monies owed mushroomed from $25,000 to just under $100,000!

"We're going in the wrong direction," I said, "even though it seems we're doing everything right."

However, we vowed to continue forging ahead. We renewed our covenant to continue giving, and we asked God for a miraculous intervention.

For sure, it was difficult. Sometimes, it felt impossible. Multiple times we had to decide if we should buy groceries or if we should tithe.

We always chose to give.

And it was during those times that some of the oddest happenstance occurrences blessed us. Those were the weeks people called and asked to take us to dinner, those were the weekends people brought boxes of groceries to our house or stocked the fridge full of meat from a hunt. Those were the times when God delivered His resources at the specific moment we needed it.

We learned, like Paul, to be content in any situation. He wrote in Philippians 4:12 (NIV): "I know what it is to be in need, and I know what it is to have plenty. I have learned the secret of being content in any and every situation, whether well fed or hungry, whether living in plenty or in want.

Even though we lived more on the "have less" side of the equation, we experienced God's power and provision.

Don't get me wrong. Many times our faith was tested tremendously.

In my earliest days of traveling with Doc, I remember riding to the airport knowing that Beverly only had $50 to get through the week. That amount would need to cover gas, food . . . everything. Somehow, she stewarded what we had and made it work.

Once I returned home and walked into an empty house. She and the kids were there, but that was it. Our living room sofa and chairs—even the television—were gone!

"Did you sell the furniture to feed the family?" I asked. "What happened?"

"No, no," she replied. "I met some missionaries who just transitioned back to the States. They didn't have any furniture, so I gave ours to them."

I thought, "Geez, now we don't have any furniture. And we don't have any money to replace it. God will have to do something, or we'll just sit on the floor."

Beverly told me, "It's handled. God is going to provide."

We sat on the floor that day. However, the next day I returned to the office to plan the next ministry trip. A furniture catalog sat on my desk.

"That's strange," I said.

I opened it and discovered a letter with a check for $2,500. Beverly was right—God had already orchestrated His provision.

"The Lord spoke to me and said you needed new furniture," I read. "I thought you and your wife would best know which furniture exactly and might enjoy picking it, so I brought you this catalog." In a moment, God replaced what we once had—and did so far better than we could have envisioned.

However, the IRS issue still lingered. Furthermore, it continued expanding!

A businessman learned about my dilemma and told me, "I think I need to help you resolve this. We need to fix it, so you can move on unhindered by it."

"It's not fixable," I told him. "I'll be old and gray by the time this thing is settled. I've talked with them multiple times. Since I'm young, they look at me and see a lifetime of earning potential. They're not budging."

"Let me try," the man said. "What harm could it do?"

He was right. Things could only improve.

With my permission, he instructed his accountant to call the IRS. They began negotiating. After a few weeks, he returned with an answer.

"$8,000," he said. "They agreed to settle your $100,000 debt for just $8,000."

The businessman instructed his accountant to write me a check for $10,000—$8,000 to pay the debt and $2,000 to cover any taxes I might incur on the gift, just to make sure I didn't find myself owing the IRS anything else from the situation! After five years of sowing and walking it out through the daily grind of life, we reaped many times over, and then saw God's intervention through that entire season of life.

The following Sunday Pastor asked me to share the story in church—as a testimony of what God does. The following day, I received a call at the office from a guy who was in church that weekend.

"I called my brother in Jacksonville," he said.

At the time, that's where the IRS offices for the State of Florida were located.

"I hear miracles and breakthroughs and other stories in church," the man continued, "and I just want to know if they're always true. My brother works for the IRS, so I called him to see if this could happen. Turns out, he's the representative who talked with the accountant."

"Oh, really! It's a small world, isn't it?"

"Yeah, I'll say. After he confirmed it was true, I asked him why he handled the case that way."

"What did he say?"

"I don't know," he replied. "That's what he said. He didn't know. But he did know that he felt compelled to do it. That's the word he used, compelled. A force led him to fix it for you."

BRING IT!

We've endeavored to model this same generosity in our church. Early on, we created a ministry (Project 58) designed to provide specifically for the poor and needy.

After a season, instead of passing an offering plate, we decided to set boxes in the back of the room. We titled the boxes "Bring it" boxes—and labeled them as such.

Rather than asking people for money—or encouraging them to give—we wanted to follow the directives of Malachi 3:10 where the prophet encouraged people to "bring all the tithes into the storehouse." Notably, he didn't "take it."

This seems to be the approach in the Bible. In 2 Kings 12 we meet King Joash. The Temple had fallen in disrepair under his predecessors, so he sought to repair it. To fund it, he told the priests to take a freewill offering. Notice how they collected the money"

> *Jehoiada the priest took a chest and bored a hole in its lid. He placed it beside the altar, on the right side as one enters the temple of the Lord. The priests who guarded the entrance put into the chest all the money that was brought to the temple of the Lord.* —2 Kings 12:9, NIV

By the way, when we set this up, there was no such thing as online giving. Smartphone apps were over a decade in the future away. People actually had to "bring it" with them—or send it in the mail. The transition required a bit more faith then than it would now! However, we saw a 20% boost in giving that first month.

GIVING IS THE TRUEST DEMONSTRATION OF SALVATION

There are a few life lessons I believe our kids truly need to grab hold of. One of these is generosity, as it taps into the character of God.

It's interesting to me that many churches think that "confessing Jesus as Lord" is the target. For certain, I want my children—and everyone's children—to affirm the Lordship of Christ. But I believe there's more that God wants to do in our lives, especially as it relates to stewardship and generosity.

Notice what we find in Matthew 7:21-23 (NIV). Jesus says:

Not everyone who says to me, 'Lord, Lord' will enter the kingdom of heaven, but only the one who does the will of my Father who is in heaven. Many will say to me on that day, 'Lord, Lord, did we not prophesy in your name and in your name drive out demons and in your name perform many miracles? Then I will tell them plainly, 'I never knew you. Away from me, you evildoers!

In this passage we see that the declaration of "Jesus as Lord," which is the one thing most ministries teach as the entrance ticket to Heaven, doesn't work. Though the confessors presumed it would, it doesn't.

In addition, many of them walked in supernatural power. They prophesied, performed miracles, and exorcised demons. They walked in the anointing, some might say.

That wasn't enough, either. In fact, Jesus referred to them as "evil doers."

It beckons the question, What's important to God?

At the end of the same Gospel, we read the story of the "sheep and the goats" (author paraphrase, Matthew 25:31-46). At the end of the age, an angel gathers everyone together and divides the crowd into two groups. The sheep are set to one side; the goats are moved to the other.

The goats are addressed second. They are told that they overlooked the Master while He walked among them—that they didn't feed him when He was hungry, they didn't clothe Him when He was naked, and they didn't visit Him while He was imprisoned.

They're shocked. They're confident they would have certainly met His needs.

But that's the point. They didn't, because "whatever you did not do for one of the least of these, you did not do for me" (Matthew 25:45, NIV).

Oddly enough, the sheep find themselves just as surprised as the goats. Instead of sending them to everlasting torment, as He did the goats (author paraphrase, Matthew 25:46), the Master welcomes them into eternal life—precisely because they fed, clothed, and visited Him. Yet they don't recall doing any of these things . . . for Him, that is.

He tells them, "Whatever you did for one of the least of these brothers and sisters of mine, you did for me" (Matthew 25:40, NIV).

Notably, they didn't do these deeds to earn it. Neither group did. If salvation was earned, we might argue that both groups would have gladly fed, clothed, and visited their King.

But it wasn't.

Generosity (or a lack of it) resulted from their heart condition. It was a natural overflow of who they were.

> **IF BOLDNESS IS THE KEY TO UNLOCKING GOD'S POWER, THEN GENEROSITY IS THE KEY TO UNLOCKING EVERYTHING ELSE.**

The prophet Jeremiah affirmed this. Writing of a noble person, he states in Jeremiah 22:16 (NIV), "'He defended the cause of the poor and needy, and so all went well. Is that not what it means to know me?' declares the Lord."

Psalm 112:6-9 (NIV) affirms that when we live generously, we not only walk into blessing, but we walk in victory. Our enemy scatters, defeated:

Surely the righteous will never be shaken; they will be remembered forever. They will have no fear of bad news; their hearts are steadfast, trusting in the Lord. Their hearts are secure, they will have no fear; in the end they will look in triumph on their foes. They have freely scattered their gifts to the poor, their righteousness endures forever; their horn will be lifted high in honor.

Doc often said, "Let's give and grieve the devil!"

I saw this in every facet of his life. He modeled it, and he revealed that if boldness is the key to unlocking God's power, then generosity is the key to unlocking everything else.

CHAPTER 8

ACTIVATION THROUGH LIVING OUT THE WORD OF GOD

One Sunday evening, Pastor Benny stepped to the mic to preach. By now, I was learning where the books of the Bible are located, and I could flip through the pages quickly.

He led the congregation to Luke 22:10. There, Jesus told the disciples to go prepare a place for them to share the Passover meal—the meal which we often refer to as the Last Supper.

"Find the man with the pitcher of water on his shoulder," Pastor Benny read.

I remember sitting—in my chair on the stage, of course—wondering, "How in the world did they know which man? People didn't have refrigerators and sinks. They made constant trips to the well. There could be dozens of men carrying water."

It was almost as if he read my mind: "I know what some of you are thinking," he said. Then—"Which one of the men?"

Heads nodded, affirming the dilemma. How would the disciples know where to go, who to approach?"

Pastor Benny continued, "In that culture, men didn't carry water. Women did."

It all made sense now. A man would have never done that job. In the odd event there was, everyone would have recognized the uniqueness of the moment.

Just as the disciples did. They clearly identified the lone man with a jug of water on his shoulder, followed him to the house, and prepared a place to share a final meal—a Passover celebration, at that—with Jesus.

I asked Pastor how he knew about this cultural issue. He told me that part of the reason is his own background—he's from Israel. The bigger factor, though, is that he invested hours mining the Scriptures for the gold buried within.

"If your Bible is falling apart, you're not," Doc often said.

He was right; he is right. It's almost as if you get to choose which one you want to be in tatters—your Bible or you.

One of the revelations I received from Pastor was to esteem the Word of God, and to invest time meeting the Lord within its pages. Many people don't know—because they've primarily seen him in crusades or healing meetings—but Pastor Benny is an incredible teacher of the

Word. Moreover, he doesn't just want people to know the Bible, but he yearns for them to know the God of the Bible.

JESUS REVEALS FINALITY IN THE PRESENT

I remember one of the first times I sat under his teaching. He took us to the book of Exodus, to the Passover.

He reminded us that God told Moses that the Children of Israel were "to take some of the blood and put it on the sides and tops of the doorframes of the houses where they eat the lambs" (Exodus 12:7, NIV).

They were told to do this in a specific manner, using a specific plant to paint the shape of a cross: "Take a bunch of hyssop, dip it into the blood in the basin and put some of the blood on the top and on both sides of the doorframe. None of you shall go out of the door of your house until morning" (Exodus 12:22, NIV).

Pastor Benny then told us, "The New Testament refers to Jesus as the Lamb of God. John the Baptist said this as He walked by one day. In John 1:29 (NKJV) he exclaimed, 'This is the Lamb of God. He is the One who takes away the sins of the world!'"

He continued, "When Jesus was first born, though, it's very interesting that the angels first delivered the message to shepherds who lived outside Jerusalem" (author paraphrase, Luke 2:8-20).

He explained that many people feel that God first appeared to the shepherds because they were of the lowest class in society and that He called the magi through the star since they were of the highest. Somehow, this might show us that Jesus came for all people—that there's no race or class or group He excludes.

"But there's a bit more happening in this passage," Pastor Benny said. "These shepherds, I believe, were the special group of shepherds who dwelled outside the Sheep Gate—just beyond the walls of Jerusalem."

The Sheep Gate was located near the Temple. A group of shepherds raised the sacrificial animals which were led to be sacrificed for the sins of the people. The shepherds made certain that only the perfect lambs, those without spot or blemish, were taken to the Temple.

"'Get the picture," he taught. "From the beginning, God appeared to that specific group of shepherds so they could certify that this was our Passover Lamb. And He was perfect."

He continued, "Then, as Jesus began His ministry, John the Baptist affirmed it!"

He highlighted Jesus' trial—how the high priest, the ruling elders, and the scribes all gathered and pronounced Jesus "guilty" (author paraphrase, John 14:53). Then, Pontius Pilate ordered Jesus to crucifixion at the "third hour" (approximately 9 a.m.) on Passover day (author paraphrase, John 15:25). You couldn't miss the parallels.

Nor could you not catch this. John reminds us of the hyssop plant, as he recounts Jesus' final statements from the Cross in John 19:28-30 (NIV):

Later, knowing that everything had now been finished, and so that Scripture would be fulfilled, Jesus said, "I am thirsty." A jar of wine vinegar was there, so they soaked a sponge in it, put the sponge on a stalk of the hyssop plant, and lifted it to Jesus' lips. When he had received the drink, Jesus said, "It is finished." With that, he bowed his head and gave up his spirit.

Pastor Benny suggested that "The declaration that 'It is finished' says so much here, too. The verb tense shows us so much about the sacrifice."

The Greek language in which John wrote expresses verbs in two tenses: the perfect tense and the imperfect tense. Whereas imperfect verbs refer to repeating actions—things you'll need to do again, such as cutting your hair, cleaning the house, or mowing the yard—perfect verbs denote finality. The thing is done.

> **WE DON'T BELIEVE GOD IN THE PRESENT BECAUSE WE READ OF EVENTS THAT OCCURRED IN THE PAST. RATHER, WE TRUST GOD IN THE PRESENT BECAUSE THE EVENTS CONTINUE OCCURRING.**

"For years the priests declared 'It is finished' whenever they offered a sacrifice," Pastor said. "This goes back to the time of Moses and the first sacrifices at the Tabernacle. But they always used an imperfect tense of the verb."

"In effect, the priests said something like, 'Yes, this is done. Your sacrifice is accepted. But you will need to sacrifice again.'"

In fact, the book of Hebrews tells us that "those sacrifices are an annual reminder of sins." We're told the reason is "because it is impossible for the blood of bulls and goats to take away sins" (John 10:3-4, NIV). Sacrifices never removed sin; they reminded worshipers that something more thorough was needed.

"When Jesus died," Pastor Benny preached, "he reminded us that Jesus took the priestly language but changed it. Rather than stating 'It is finished' in the imperfect tense, He used the perfect tense. He emphasized that the payment for sin—all sin past, present, and future—was handled."

But how does He know?

As I heard him preach like that so many times, I pondered, "How does he know all of this? How does he make these connections?"

But as I traveled with him I discovered why: he saturated himself with the Word of God. For instance, it was not uncommon to find him asleep with the Bible next to him. It might be the final thing he saw as he drifted to sleep, as well as the first thing he held when he awoke—right as he greeted the Holy Spirit with his customary, "Good morning!"

Today, you can walk through a Christian bookstore or scan the Bible section at the local Barnes & Noble and find numerous types of study Bibles. They sell versions with cultural notes, editions with pages for journaling, and color coordinated guides which highlight different verses based on what the words emphasize.

Before these study Bibles were available, though, Doc created his own. If you flip through his Bible you'll find untold layers of notices and penciled-in cross-references. And, you'll see some color coding.

He loves colored pencils. He showed me how he chose certain colors to remind him of specific things. For instance, red might refer to prophecy. Green might reference a promise. Yellow denotes Jesus and His Lordship.

Even though I haven't served on his staff in a few decades, we still speak regularly. Not too long ago he mentioned he was learning the Hebrew language.

"Why are you learning Hebrew?" I asked.

"Because of the Word of God. I want to read the Old Testament in the original language—in case there's something I've missed."

"What do you mean? You've read it through so many times."

"Yes, but perhaps there's a deeper insight I will see through the nuances of the language."

I marveled. Here he is in his 70s. Yet he's still confident there are many more layers of gold to find in the Scripture.

Once when many people ceased following Jesus, He looked to the twelve and asked if they wanted to leave Him also. Peter's answer in John 6:68 reminds me of Doc.

"To whom would we go," he said. "You have the words of life!"

In our day, so many people debate whether certain stories in the Bible really occurred. Did God really create the world in seven days? Were Adam and Eve real people? Did He really move the Red Sea so the Children of Israel could walk through on dry land?

To me—and I learned this from Pastor Benny, because I didn't know much about the Bible when I met him (I was a new Christian)—I'm so far beyond those questions. The Bible isn't just a book and facts and figures with which we mentally assent. That is, we don't believe God in the present because we read of events that occurred in the past. Rather, we trust God in the present because the events continue occurring.

Or, to say it another way, "We don't believe because it happened, we believe because it happens."

That is—

God called men like Abraham, telling them it was okay to leave a pagan homeland. God had a plan for him and his family and would do something wonderful through them if they agreed to start over (author paraphrase, Genesis 12:1).

God worked through men like Joseph, the man who was raised in a dysfunctional family. God not only restored that family, He blessed nations in the process (author paraphrase, Genesis 50:20).

God touched people like the woman who spent all she had on physicians but never got better through those efforts. Actually, she got worse—until she met Jesus and was healed (author paraphrase, Mark 5:25-29).

God called Lazarus—who was dead—to rise and come back to life (author paraphrase, John 11:43).

He still moves today. In all of these ways. And more.

THE CATCH TO RECEIVING REVELATION

But you can only walk in the revelation you've received. And the starting point is to create space where God can move.

Note what David wrote in Psalm 119: 11-16 (NIV):

I have hidden your word in my heart that I might not sin against you. Praise be to you, Lord; teach me your decrees. With my lips I recount all the laws that come from your mouth. I rejoice in following your statutes as one rejoices in great riches. I meditate on your precepts and consider your ways. I delight in your decrees; I will not neglect your word.

God didn't hide the Word in David's heart on autopilot; David hid it. Sure, the Holy Spirit illuminated that Word—and gave Him recall and additional revelation. However, to put it in "Doc terms," David fell asleep with the Word, he developed his color-coding system as he read, and he read and re-read those Scriptures over and over in hopes that he might see yet another facet of his Redeemer.

Doc didn't place many rules on his staff. When we traveled for the crusades, he had one he insisted upon, though.

"Only read the Bible," he instructed us.

That was it. No magazines. No newspapers. No television.

"Consecrate yourselves in the Word," he encouraged us.

YOU WILL COME TO KNOW HIM . . . IN TIME

One day when I was working for Pastor Benny we were talking as I drove him to the airport. I found myself continually staggered by his knowledge of the Bible. Honestly, when I would sit there as a young believer under his teachings, my mind was blown with the spirit of revelation that would move in and through him.

That day, I asked him, "Doc, how do you know the Bible so well? How are you able to communicate the truth of Scripture so powerfully?"

He said, "Mattox, it's just time. If you'll just keep studying the Scriptures, just keep reading the Bible, and just be faithful in studying the Word of God, I'm going to tell you what will happen to you . . . "

After a pause, he added:

Here's what will happen. One day, years from now, somebody's going to drive you to the airport just like you're doing for me today. They're going to look and ask, 'How do you know the Bible so well? How are you able to communicate the truth of Scripture so powerfully?' They'll ask you the same question you just asked me.

So that's exactly what I did. I gave my life to the study of God's Word, then to faithfully communicating what I saw in Scripture.

His Word became a lamp unto my feet and a light unto my path (author paraphrase, Psalm 119:105). His Word influenced all my decisions and made crooked paths straight (author paraphrase, Proverbs

3:5-6). His Word has been sweet as honey (author paraphrase, Psalm 119:103). I've seen, firsthand, the power and protection His Word offers—His Word is life (author paraphrase, John 6:68).

And do you know what happened?

It was recent. I forgot all about that conversation until one day a young man who had come through our recovery program drove me to the airport.

We were talking and, at some point in the conversation, just like Doc said, the driver asked, "Pastor Kent, how do you know so much of the Bible? How are you able to communicate the truths of Scripture so powerfully?"

I immediately burst into tears. It must have been shocking for the young man, but I was instantly taken back to the time, years ago, when I drove Doc to the airport. Now, I was living that moment he said I would experience.

I dried me eyes and told the man the whole story. Then, I added, "If you'll just keep studying the Scriptures, just keep reading the Bible, and just be faithful to studying the Word of God, the same thing is going to happen to you."

PART 3
ONWARD

CHAPTER 9

CHARTING YOUR NEXT CHAPTER

The Lord writes our story for us, and that story always involves chapters. There comes a time when the Lord will turn the page. It does not mean you were in the wrong place; it means that you cannot take that place with you to the next chapter. This is where Beverly and I find ourselves today—in a different chapter. Your previous chapters will always provide sufficient context for your next one.

Dad's business did quite well in Orlando. Remember, we moved there in the 80s.

Walt Disney World was just down the road. It wasn't on the map then in the same way it is now, but the Kissimmee area where we were located was already bustling with hotels, restaurants, and attractions.

Dad built a large Go-Kart and putt-putt amusement center which rode the oncoming wave of growth, providing substantial salaries for him and his business partner each year. Then, after about seven years, he cashed out, selling his share of the business.

He walked away a millionaire, now holding a nest egg with which he could retire. When he signed the papers for that deal, it was as if the Lord—in a moment—returned to him the years the locusts had eaten (author paraphrase, Joel 2:25).

Yes, we were blessed, too. Just like he said would happen. It was a much different—and better—blessing than we imagined was possible. But such is the nature of God!

IF, THEN . . .

He and my mother moved back to Alabama. Beverly and I weren't ready to leave Florida. We knew our time there was coming to a close, thatced the Lord was re-directing us into a ministry of our own, but it wasn't quite time.

I remember telling the Lord, "I can't wait to preach!"

In fact, I grew anxious for the opportunity. I became discouraged. I grew tired of the waiting. In my thinking, I had invested ten years in *not* preaching—even though I felt that was what I was called to do, even though Beverly had shared that crazy vision she had when driving her car before she was saved.

God told me, "Son, I promise, there will come a day when you will have preached so many times that it won't matter to you whether you will preach again!"

At the time I couldn't imagine that ever happening—and I'm still not there! However, the Lord certainly made good on that promise!

To be honest, I got antsy during the waiting. I remember one night when the Holy Spirit corrected me on this. I was on an airplane flying by myself. During that season I served our crusade team, and they had all returned home from London. I sat in the seat at 30,000 feet feeling alone and exhausted.

"I can't keep doing this," I thought.

The Holy Spirit quickened my spirit and led me to Philippians 2.

"Read it," the Spirit said.

I slowly walked my way through the familiar passage. I saw the admonition that began with a big IF (Philippians 2:1-2, NIV): "Therefore if you have any encouragement from being united with Christ, if any comfort from his love, if any common sharing in the Spirit, if any tenderness and compassion, then make my joy complete by being like-minded, having the same love, being one in spirit and of one mind."

> **IT HIT ME: IF MY LORD JESUS WILLINGLY TOOK THE FORM OF SERVANTHOOD, I CERTAINLY COULD AS WELL.**

The fact is that I absolutely did have encouragement from my oneness with Jesus. And I certainly felt like I was sharing in His Spirit.

I knew, in that moment, that I should be like-minded—as verse 2 suggested.

I continued reading and it hit me anew: "He made himself nothing by taking the very nature of a servant" (Philippians 2:7, NIV).

It hit me: if my Lord Jesus willingly took the form of servanthood, I certainly could as well. I settled it in my heart. I could continue serving.

"If this is what you want me to do for the rest of my life, I'll do it," I prayed.

LEARNING TO FLY

It wasn't too long after that when I received a call to go to a church.

I asked the Lord, "Is this of you? Should I go?"

"It's not me," the Lord replied. He reminded me of the lessons I learned about submission and authority. "Your time is coming. But if this was of Me, I would have told Pastor Benny as well."

I decided to wait. I could continue serving—just as I affirmed on the flight back home.

A few weeks later, Doc called me to his office and told me, "Mattox, I think it's time for you to start preaching some. Maybe go out once a month."

Immediately, I began receiving invitations to churches at exactly that rate—once per month. It was never more, it was never less.

After a season, Doc approached me with another admonition: "You're handling this very well. Why don't you go twice a month?"

Instantly, the invitations doubled. Again, they never exceeded twice a month, yet it was always exactly that. It was almost like manna from

Heaven—just what I needed, one day at a time (author paraphrase, Exodus 16:1-36, Matthew 6:11).

GOD'S TRANSITIONS ARE ALWAYS ON TIME

During this season I continued serving Pastor Benny while also learning how to work on my own. It was a great balance, because I was able to step out a little at a time.

I remember serving with him in South Africa one week. I had been with him for a decade. The Lord woke me one morning around six o'clock.

The Lord said, "Over the next ten years you will travel the earth. Your family will be by your side, and your strength will not fail you." He added, "It's time to leave Pastor and go do what I've called you to do."

I knew it was the Lord. I also knew that He would confirm it if it was Him.

After traveling 250 days each year for ten years without my wife—who raised our kids, ran our household, and is the real hero—I knew it was time for us to serve together, side-by-side. I looked forward to that next chapter.

Yet I still had questions. How do I address this? Who all needs to know? Should I bring it up or wait for Pastor Benny to bring it up?

I thought about this and prayed for a few hours. Then, I went to the crusade location for a soundcheck. Our sound man approached me crying.

"Are you okay?" I asked.

"Yeah," he replied. "This isn't about me—it's about you."

"What do you mean?"

He explained, "The glory of the Lord filled my room this morning around 6 a.m. It was so thick I had to get out of the bed and lie on the floor."

"What was God talking to you about?" I asked.

"He told me to tell you to follow through on what He told you to do this morning."

I knew the transition was about to happen. I recognized the pattern in the Bible. In fact, Doc had taught me about it. With your spiritual leader you always walk through a progression from Bethel (the place of revelation and learning, author paraphrase, Genesis 28:10-22) to Jericho (the place of war, of doing the ministry, author paraphrase, Joshua 6:1-27) to the Jordan (the place you cross back over on your own, author paraphrase, 2 Kings 2:8,14).

THE OFFER OF A LIFETIME

Pastor Benny, knowing it was time, told me, "I don't want you to get out there and struggle. You've been so faithful to me."

He outlined a plan.

This is what I would like to do for you. I want to book you in the largest churches in each area where we hold a crusade—before and after our meetings. That way you'll get known and build a reputation. You can just work for me one week a month, and I'll continue paying you full time. We'll take care of your benefits, too.

He continued, "After a few years, you will have built a strong ministry, and you can step into the next chapter."

Doc would have taken care of me. The offer was phenomenally generous. Like I said, he is one of the most giving people I know. And this shows the heart of a true spiritual father.

I took it to the Lord in prayer.

The Lord asked me:

Do you want Doc to supply you and build your ministry, or do you want Me to build it? Elisha eventually left Elijah. Joshua eventually left Moses. Now is your time to leave Pastor Benny. Go honor him and tell him that you love him—and thank him for being so gracious. But you have to make a choice."

Doc offered a clear path that was paved. Everything was provided for.

I knew, though, as kind as the invitation was, that I had to trust the Lord.

A TIME TO REAP

From the moment I left, Beverly and I began reaping all the seeds sown from the previous years. Remember, that's how submission works.

We didn't send any letters or make any phone calls. By that time I knew thousands of pastors I could have called.

We had an answering machine and a telephone. I love popcorn, and we had two empty popcorn canisters—the kind you get around Christmas. The answering machine sat on one; the telephone sat on the other.

I told the Lord, "Okay, you know the number. You know where we're located. If you want us to go somewhere, show them how to reach us."

One morning while we were drinking coffee, that phone rang. I could hardly believe it. I mean, yes, I witnessed hundreds of miracles during my ten years with Pastor Benny, but this was different. Now I was the one responsible.

The first time the phone rang, the caller asked, "How often does Pastor Benny let you go out and preach?"

"Well, that's what I'm doing now. I've stepped out on my own."

"Really? Well, you can come to North Carolina and preach for me, then!"

That was the first stop. Of many. From the time we left to visit that church, we continued receiving invitation after invitation. We physically circled the entire globe without initiating a phone call and without sending a query letter.

IN CASE IT DOESN'T WORK OUT . . . BUT IT DID

Eventually, after another decade, we knew it was time to stop traveling. That had been the word of the Lord to us.

Though I'd watched Doc build a church and then grow a traveling ministry from within it, I sensed the Lord had the opposite approach for us. We would stop traveling and build a home base.

At the time a group of eight of us regularly gathered to pray. What did God have in mind for us?

We felt like we were called to plant a church. The only problems were that we didn't know how to start one and, even if we did, we didn't have a place to meet.

"You can use some of this land," my dad said. "I'm not giving it to you—I'll sell it. But you don't have to pay me in advance for it."

When I was sixteen, I lived on that same land. I remember showering one day and making a decision to walk away from the Lord. I would pursue life on my terms.

Of course, you know how that went. I found myself battling addictions, shackled with debt, and working through too many other issues to count.

As dad offered the land, I saw—yet again—the providence of God. He brought me back, full circle, right where I began. I was given the opportunity to start anew. This time, however, God had blessed me. Even though I took the long way to travel from where I was to where I was destined to be, He had been faithful.

Anyway, dad offered me some advice about the property. "Go borrow money against the land to erect a building where you can all meet." Then—"Just don't make it look like church. That way, if it doesn't work out, you can always sell it or do something else with it."

That sounded reasonable.

This was an answered prayer, but now we needed to decide what it should look like. "Not like a church" leaves much to the architect's discretion. And we weren't sure what size it needed to be. At that time, we could all fit around the dinner table.

"Build for 500," the Lord told us in prayer.

That sounded like a big number. There were only 20,000 people living in the Oxford city limits at the time—and we were about five miles down the interstate from that. Sure, there were people scattered across the countryside, dwelling in the outlying areas, but there were not massive housing developments.

"500," the Lord affirmed.

Person after person in our group confirmed it, so we began drawing plans for a metal warehouse-looking structure that could seat 500 worshipers. And, since we had no money, we leveraged the equity of the land to make it happen.

All those months the construction crews worked on that site, I wondered, "How in the world are we going to let 500 people know about this?"

It was the year 2000. The Internet existed—people had been certain Y2K was going to bring the World Wide Web, as well as just about everything digital, down in an instant.

Social media didn't yet exist. Text messaging was rare. The houses were too far apart to go walking the neighborhoods, knocking on doors.

How would everyone learn about our new church?

Then what seemed to be a crisis happened. Two days before we received keys to our new building, my dad died. Our very first service in the new building was my dad's funeral.

Turns out, Dad was well loved. People from across the area, many of them non-church goers, came to pay their respects. Each one of them found themselves sitting in the sanctuary of our new church.

Yes, the first worship service in our church building was a funeral. Every seat—all 500—was full.

Moreover, dad's send-off was much like Samson making a final, well-calculated blow against the enemy. In the same way the infamous judge of Israel exerted more devastation to the enemy in his death than he did throughout his entire life (see Judges 16:30), so also did my father push down walls of darkness and oppression and release the power and presence of God in the area.

The week before His death, Jesus told the disciples that He too had to die. He declared in John 12:24 (NIV): "Very truly I tell you, unless a kernel of wheat falls to the ground and dies, it remains only a single seed. But if it dies, it produces many seeds."

We saw the fruit of dad's life continue bearing fruit in the same way. Everyone who has walked through the doors of Word Alive over the past 20+ years, every person who has been touched through Project 58, the recovery center, and the All in Alabama movement are all, in a direct way, part of the harvest that continues bearing fruit.

The life and ministry I continue to enjoy, the benefits and the blessings I receive, and the anointing I carry all directly connect to these revelations and the time I spent serving my dear friend—and spiritual father—Pastor Benny Hinn.

THE REVELATIONS

So, here we are. These are the seven revelations I received from Doc, my spiritual father:

1) The revelation of the supernatural—how the presence of Heaven really is available here on earth.
2) The revelation of boldness—and how walking in it is the key to experiencing the power of God.
3) The revelation of the Holy Spirit as person—and how He really wants us to know Him and interact with Him in each facet of life.
4) The revelation of worship—and how everything really is about Jesus.
5) The revelation of the power of submission—and how God gifts us human relationships to pass on the greatest lessons and empowerments of the Kingdom while also protecting us.
6) The revelation of generosity—and how we walk in the very character of the God who loves the world so much that He gave His Son when we live with open hands.
7) The revelation of the Word of God—and how God has given us a written record of His past revelation so that we might have guardrails as guide lights as we walk in communion with Him.

As I reflect on my story I'm astounded that God plucked a young man from Alabama who disavowed Him, introduced him to a girl from North Carolina who had two kilos of cocaine in her trunk, transplanted them to Orlando, called them out during a worship service using a man who moved to the United States from Israel, took us around the globe for over a decade, and then brought us back to my home. In some way, I feel that part of the reason for all of that was to write this book, and impart these same revelations to you.

Doc imparted them to me, and my prayer is that through this book they've been transferred to you—so that you may continue passing them to others.

RESOURCES

THE ART AND THEOLOGY OF LEADERSHIP

Find more resources to empower you to walk into your full leadership potential at www.LifeOfFreedom.site/LEAD.

Whether you're looking for books, courses to help you take a deeper dive, audio you can stream on-the-go, or even 1:1 coaching to help you reach your full potential, we can help!

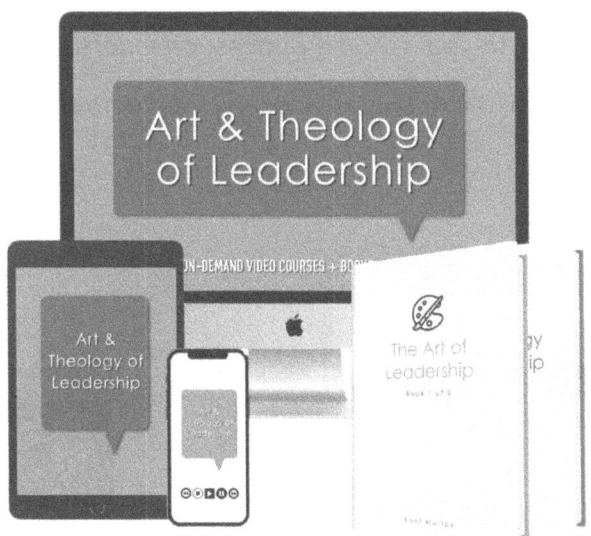

THE FREEDOM PODCAST

The Freedom Podcast is one of the best ways to connect with #TeamFreedom and the movement we're stepping into.

Each week Kent and Beverly sit down and talk about "all things freedom," highlighting some of the unique facets of:

FRIENDS—and Kingdom-connections (we weren't designed to do this alone).

FUN—because the life God calls us to IS ABSOLUTELY an adventure (and, sometimes, that's putting it mildly).

FAITH—it IS all about Jesus and what He has done for us in the past, promises to do in the future, and walks us through in the present.

We upload new episodes every Tuesday morning and then push the content from our website to your favorite podcast providers.

Find all the details at https://www.lifeoffreedom.site/podcasts/freedom-podcast

THE TRANSFORMATION COMMUNITY

Receive member's only training through the Hebrew calendar + bonus resources and insights from Kent and Beverly reserved exclusively for the Transformation Community.

Details at www.LifeOfFreedom.site/community

THE TRANSFORMATION COMMUNITY

www.ingramcontent.com/pod-product-compliance
Lightning Source LLC
Chambersburg PA
CBHW070545090426
42735CB00013B/3074